DARK PSYCHOLOGY

Learn How to Recognize Mind Control Best Techniques

(The Guide to Knowing the Strategies of a Successful Persuader)

Maxine Biondo

Published By Phil Dawson

Maxine Biondo

All Rights Reserved

Dark Psychology: Learn How to Recognize Mind Control Best Techniques (The Guide to Knowing the Strategies of a Successful Persuader)

ISBN 978-1-77485-347-4

All rights reserved. No part of this guide may be reproduced in any form without permission in writing from the publisher except in the case of brief quotations embodied in critical articles or reviews.

Legal & Disclaimer

The information contained in this book is not designed to replace or take the place of any form of medicine or professional medical advice. The information in this book has been provided for educational and entertainment purposes only.

The information contained in this book has been compiled from sources deemed reliable, and it is accurate to the best of the Author's knowledge; however, the Author cannot guarantee its accuracy and validity and cannot be held liable for any errors or omissions. Changes are periodically made to this book. You must consult your doctor or get professional medical advice before using any of the suggested remedies, techniques, or information in this book.

Upon using the information contained in this book, you agree to hold harmless the Author from and against any damages, costs, and expenses, including any legal fees potentially resulting from the application of any of the information provided by this guide. This disclaimer applies to any damages or injury caused by the use and application, whether directly or indirectly, of any advice or information presented, whether for breach of contract, tort, negligence, personal injury, criminal intent, or under any other cause of action.

You agree to accept all risks of using the information presented inside this book. You need to consult a professional medical practitioner in order to ensure you are both able and healthy enough to participate in this program.

TABLE OF CONTENTS

INTRODUCTION 1

CHAPTER 1: WHAT IS DARK PSYCHOLOGY? 5

CHAPTER 2: DARK PERSONALITY AND DARK TRIAD: MACHIAVELLIANISM NARCISSISM, PSYCHOPATHY 13

CHAPTER 3: DARK PSYCHOLOGY STRATEGIES 27

CHAPTER 4: ART OF PERSUASION 44

CHAPTER 5: DECEIT BEYOND THE LITTLE WHITE LIE 58

CHAPTER 6: WHAT IS THE DARK TRIAD? 71

CHAPTER 7: MANIPULATION THEORIES 93

CHAPTER 8: WHAT IS EMOTIONAL MANIPULATION? 117

CHAPTER 9: THE ART OF BRAINWASHING, AND OTHER MIND CONTROL STRATEGIES 135

CHAPTER 10: UTILIZING NLP (NLP) TO INFLUENCE PEOPLE 154

CHAPTER 11: WHAT IS BRAINWASHING WORKS 172

CONCLUSION 183

Introduction

In the present it is essential to be aware of manipulators. If you are able to recognize when somebody is trying influence you It will be more easy to escape their grasp.

Once you are able to discern the signs of manipulation, how it manifests and the way it has impacted your life, it will be simpler to avoid it. Engaging with others could mean making every effort to stay away from it. However, preventing yourself from being controlled isn't the only significant thing we'll be discussing.

We will pay a lot of focus on how you can be an effective person for yourself. Although you may have suffered in the past due to manipulation, or worse, affected your mental health being a manipulator but there is hope today, that we can strive towards a better life for us. It is achieved by being an inspiring and possibly influential individual.

Manipulation can be dangerous, but when it is seen in a positively, then it could be a healthy influence.

If you can be persuasive and not just get your desired items, but also meet the desires of others It will be more simple to allow you to achieve the things you would like most in life.

Instead of doing everything you don't like, becoming your own "yes guy," or letting people benefit from your great personality, you could be equally influential as people who attempted to control you before.

You may even be at a point that you're afraid of manipulating completely. What would make you want to perform something which has resulted in your suffering before? This type of thinking happens because we've only been conscious of the negative forms of manipulative behavior. But, it is crucial to make sure that we have the tools needed for understanding how to acquire these types of information.

The initial step is to research the different personality types of manipulators and also those they typically pursue. There is a chance that you have heard about the most common personality kind, "Narcissist," a person who is focused on his own needs and obtaining the things they want. Narcissists can benefit from empaths, or individuals who're more concerned about the health of other people.

In the next section, we will look at positive manipulative personalities as well as how you can apply some of these beneficial techniques in your own relationships.

In addition we'll be examining the way our bodies communicate through the body, the messages and reactions that we emit and the things that others could be getting by our bodies. The more you know about influence via other methods than our spoken communication the easier it will be to stay from being affected by yourself and to convince those who are around you.

When we have a clear understanding of what this all means it will be much simpler to understand and implement the other key techniques we'll be sharing throughout the book.

Although it may seem easy to manipulate people negatively from whom you wish to get some thing, the person you'd be most hurt during this process is likely to be yourself.

Always try to find ways of positive influence, so that you are able to benefit both sides.

Chapter 1: What is Dark Psychology?

Our definition defines Dark Psychology as the art and science that focuses on manipulation of the mind and control. Psychology, in a broad term, is a way of researching and understanding the behavior of humans. It focuses on our actions, thoughts and how we interact with one another. The dark psychology is focused on the kind of actions and thoughts that are prey-like in the nature. Dark psychology analyzes the strategies employed by criminals to persuade, motivate, influence, or force people to act in ways which are advantageous to them but could be detrimental to others.

The most accurate definition of dark psychology is involves the investigation of human's condition in relation to the person's psychological disposition to savage others. All humanity has the potential to harm not just their peers, but also other living things. While some people may wish to subdue or thwart this behavior, there are people who decide to follow these urges. What dark psychology is trying to accomplish is to help it possible to understand the thoughts of thoughts, feelings, and emotions that lead to the sexy behavior of humans. Dark psychology believes that this kind of production has specific reasons and has an underlying rational motive that is goal-oriented most of the time. The remaining time is mostly the risky abuse of others without any purpose. This is because we are able to define and perceive it by religious beliefs or evolutionary sciences.

The purpose of dark psychology as a field is to comprehend the thoughts as well as feelings and perceptions that make people behave in ways that are predatory towards one others. Psychologists working in dark psychology operate with the idea that the majority of predatory behaviors are deliberate. This means that the majority of those who prey upon others

(99.99 percent) do so to fulfill a particular reason, while those who do not (0.01 percent) are doing it without any motive whatsoever.

It is believed that when people do bad actions, they have certain motives. Some of these might even be rational in their own perspective. People commit crimes with a specific goal in mind and specific reasons for their actions. However, only a small portion of the population systematically hurts people without any motive which can be understood by evolutionary science or a type of faith-based doctrine.

There are many instances that every person has an element of darkness. Every religion and culture recognize the dark side of people to some degree. We refer the dark side as "evil" and some societies and religions have gone as that they have created mythological beings they consider to be this evil (the Satan, the devil Satan demons, etc.). Psychologists from dark psychology believe that there are a few among us who are guilty of the most heinous types of sin, for reasons that are not known. While the majority of people will engage in evil in order to attain power, wealth as a form of retribution or for sexual reasons However, there are people who do the wrong thing because they are. They commit crimes of terror without any reason. Also the ends they pursue aren't justifiable and they do harm to themselves.

Dark psychology has its roots in four dark personality traits. These are Narcissism Machiavellianism psychopathy, Machiavellianism and sadism. People who have these traits tend to be in ways that can be detrimental to others.

The methods and techniques used for manipulating others can be different. They can be utilized to gain a positive effect and also for various types of fraud. The traits of those who are able to influence others, regardless of what the "dark" within the name of dark psychology.

The people who have succeeded in using dark psychology are aware of the various aspects that are normal in psychology. They are able to understand their own behavior as well as those within their own group. They can easily assess others' opinions by using this technique. They are able to discern opinions of others, their opinions, and even other details from people they would like to influence. This skill is a skill that can be developed on their own.

Certain stories of deceitful citizens using dark psychology, such as the ones that were mentioned in the first chapter of this book were seen as being a little out of the ordinary and the people who suffered from this type of deceit were seen as endless simplicities. The majority of the fraudulent "exploits" that used the dark psychology method as a particular mental state were not even connected as the person who was suffering from dark psychological influences did not have a reason to explain what transpired.

It has been said numerous times that the particulars of dark psychology make the person who is active "process" his client's information in a loop. He doesn't issue direct commands to perform the opposite, but instead allows the person to do it as if taking the initiative. The person asks questions, comments for advice, asks questions and finally is able to get his way.

The reason for his actions is an unorthodox strategy. One of the strategies is speculation. The term is used in a manner that an event, idea, or object is presented as if it's actually accepted. For instance, they might will ask: "Will you pay in bitcoins or dollars?" The question is unintentional, but you've not yet stated that you are planning to buy the item. The inquiry assumes that you've already made an option and you are left to resolve the tiniest issue question of whether to pay with dollars or bitcoins, on which you think.

I'm guessing that what was said caused the reader to smile an ironic smile. It's an old trick, evident in the sense that it is visible by eyes that are not blind. Don't make rash conclusions. Remind yourself that since the "seller" was already adapted to you and is leading you to believe that your mind isn't as critical when you read these phrases. This is the reason for analysing people first, and then taking a step ahead including their own reactions and actions.

The basic idea behind this method is that The dark psychologist takes the language of the suggestion and after that "dissolves" the suggestion into an unrelated story. During the exchange"the "user" in ways selects the words that suggest them and they can turn out to be a fantastic method of capturing consciousness. The user (or or she) will alter the volume of the conversation and pause at certain places as well as increase or decrease the pace of the narrative.

Other tools are available to highlight the words and phrases to keep them within the mind. The "user" is able to emphasize certain areas of the story by using gestures or facial expressions, and even touching your shoulder, arm or back. He could approach you with a sharp stance and then move away, etc. These tricks when you are following these rules, form the foundation of psychological darkness. Let's consider how often it happens to us at will. This new information will help you change your life. However, before that, it's worthwhile to consider the many personalities you need to be prepared to meet...

Chapter 2: Dark Personality and Dark Triad: Machiavellianism Narcissism, Psychopathy

Dark psychology isn't an all-encompassing, universally valid medical diagnosis that is used in all instances of deviant personality. There is, in actual fact numerous ways that dark psychology could manifest in an individual's psychological and physical appearance. There isn't a definitive distinction of one personality type from another, and a variety of individuals with distinctive characteristics of dark psychology might exhibit aspects of multiple manifestations of dark psychology.

This chapter will look at three kinds of dark psychology people.

It is vital to remember that even though the internet has brought about an explosion of problems caused by the dark side of psychology, such characteristics are a part of our culture since the beginning of time. Indeed one of the darker psychology characteristics we'll be exploring during this article, Machiavellianism is named after the name of a medieval politician. Anotherone, narcissism, gets its name from a mythological character. mythological character. Together, the three dark psychology profiles discussed in this chapter--psychopathy, Machiavellianism, and narcissism--make up what is known as "the Dark Triad."

Psychopathy

Psychopathy is described as a mental disorder with a variety of defining characteristics , including antisocial behavior, amorality the inability to form meaningful relationships extreme egocentricity, as well as repeat violations that result from an inability to recognize the consequences of past mistakes. The antisocial behavior, as a result is defined as a behavior that is motivated by breaking the rules of formal or informal of social behavior by engaging in criminal activities or actions of private, personal protest or opposition, or even towards other people or society as a whole.

Egocentricity is a behavior that occurs when the person who is committing the offense sees themselves as the center of the universe or at the very least, of all the dominant actions in politics and society. Empathy is the capacity to perceive and interpret things, thoughts, emotions and convictions in the eyes of others and is thought to be to be one of the key psychological factors in establishing effective long-term relationships.

Morality is completely different from morality. Immoral acts are an act that is in violation of established moral guidelines. Someone who is morally wrong is able to confront the consequences of his or her actions in the expectation that will realize that the actions are offensive from an ethical, but not legally-based perspective. Morality, on the contrary side, is a psychological concept that doesn't recognize any moral codes exist or if they doexist, that they have no significance in determining whether to behave in one manner or the other.

Someone who is exhibiting psychopathy might commit horrendous actions which cause immense physical and mental trauma, and never be able to comprehend what they've committed is not right.

And, the people who exhibit symptoms of psychopathy tend to get worse as time passes because they are incapable of making connections between the issues that affect their lives as well as the lives of others around them , and their own destructive and harmful actions.

Machiavellianism

Machiavellianism, as it is defined in its strictest sense, is an ideology of political thought developed by Niccolo Machiavelli which was a prominent figure from 1469 to 1527, in Italy. In modern society Machiavellianism has become a word used to describe the common perception of those who are thought to have extremely high levels of ambitions in their professional or political lives. In the field of psychology the scale of Machiavellianism is utilized to gauge the extent of people who have problematic personalities exhibit manipulative behavior.

Machiavelli wrote The Prince, a political treatise that he wrote in which he argued that honesty, sincerity, as well as other qualities were wonderful qualities, but in politics, the capability to deceive or bribery as well as other kinds of criminal behavior could be tolerated if there was no other options to achieve goals in order to safeguard ones' interests.

Many misconceptions limit this method to the idea that "the goal is more important than the method." For honest, Machiavelli himself insisted that the most important element of this equation was making sure that the purpose of the process must first be justifiable.

It is also better to accomplish this goal by using methods that are not bribed when possible, since there is lesser risk to the interests of the person who is involved.

Therefore, seeking the most efficient method of achieving a goal is not always the most dangerous. Furthermore there are a variety of political goals that are deemed to be worthy of pursuing should be pursued. In some cases just a threat specific course of action could be pursued might be sufficient to get there. In other cases the treason could be as easy as offering a credible threat to do something that's not actually intended.

In our modern society most people do not realize how Machiavellianism forms part of the "Dark Triad" of dark psychology. They accept in tacitly the sinister behavior of politicians as well as business executives who have the ability to accumulate power or fortune. But, as a mental disorder, Machiavellianism is entirely different from a path chosen for political power.

The person with Machiavellian characteristics does not take into consideration whether his or her choices are an efficient method to achieve the goals he or she is seeking and if there are other options that don't require deceit or shady tactics or if the final outcome of their actions is worthy of achieving. The Machiavellian persona is not an indication of a calculated or strategic mind that is trying to reach an objective that is worthwhile in a tense context. Instead, it's always in the forefront, regardless of whether the circumstances call to take a harsh, rational and manipulative approach or not.

For instance, we've been all sick and called in to work , when we simply wanted a day off. However, for the majority of us, this isn't the way we act normally. Consequently, after actions of dishonesty, a lot of us feel ashamed. People who exhibit the highest level of Machiavellianism do not lie just because they need a break They see lying and deceit as the only method to behave regardless of whether it will bring any benefits.

Furthermore, due to the amount of acceptance by society and the implicit approval given to Machiavellian individuals who achieve the status of a politician, their presence within the society is not subject to the same negative attention that is given to the two other people in the Dark Triad: psychopathy and narcissism.

Narcissism

The expression "narcissism" is derived from an old Greek myth of Narcissus who was a young man who looked at the reflection of himself in a lake of water and became infatuated with the reflection of him. In the field of clinical psychology, narcissism as a disorder was first recognized by Sigmund Freud. Since then, it has been added to official diagnostic manuals to describe of a specific kind of psychosis.

In psychology, narcissism has been defined as a mental disorder that is that is characterized by an over-inflated sense of importance, an over desire for attention as well as an absence of empathy and as a result of this, unbalanced relationships. Most often, narcissists exhibit a high degree of confidence, however the reality is that they have an extremely fragile self-image and an extremely sensitive to criticism. There's often a huge gap between a person's highly positive perception of him or herself, and the expectation that others will offer them favors or extra treatment, and disappointment when the outcomes are rather negative or other than positive. These issues can impact every aspect that a narcissist's life is concerned which includes personal relationships, professional relationships and financial issues.

In the Dark Triad, those who have traits that stem from Narcissistic personality disorder (NPD) might be in relationships marked by inability to empathize. For instance, a narcissist might demand constant praise and attention from the person they are with however, they are often unresponsive or unable to express appreciation by showing interest or responding to the worries, thoughts, or emotions of their companion.

Narcissists also exhibit an egocentric view and seek out a lot of reward and attention, but typically never having ever done anything that can justify these sentiments. They also have the tendency to criticize excessively of the people around him or her, as well as an increased sensitivity to even the tiniest bit or criticism directed towards the person.

Narcissism in popular culture is usually portrayed as a derogatory phrase and a slur directed at those like actors or models, as well as other stars who exhibit the highest levels of self-love or fulfillment, NPD is actually a psychological term that is different from having a an impressive self-esteem.

The primary way to comprehend this dark psychological aspect is to recognize that the narcissist's perception of themselves is usually completely and totally unrealistic, extravagant and overinflated, and it is unable to be justified using any actual real accomplishments, or capabilities which could make the claims plausible. Due to the conflict between expectations and reality the manipulative, demanding and self-centered, inconsiderate and arrogant behaviour of the individual who is a narcissist may cause trouble not only for him as a person, but also for all the people who are who are in their lives.

The Dark Triad in Practice

The workplace of the professional has recognized the presence of those who exhibit Dark Triad characteristics. The diagram below illustrates how they are admired because of their efficiency and ability to accomplish their tasks however it also highlights the negative impact it can have in their capacity to build personal relationships:

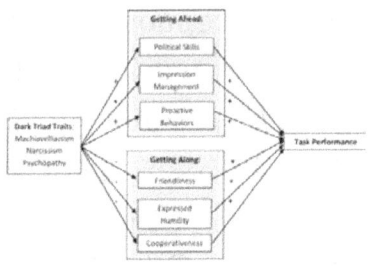

(McLarty, 2015)

The rest of the book focuses on a variety of individuals and situations which you could encounter either one or two or all three or any combination of the three Dark Triad personalities working in harmony all around you.

Clinical descriptions of the disorder are simple to classify and when taken in alone, it's quite simple to distinguish one kind of dark psychology from another. The reality is much more complicated. A lot of us have become comfortable with so-called "toxic relations," whether they are relationships with our spouses as well as our coworkers, families, the bosses of our employers or our local and political leaders. Additionally, the manifestations of dark psychological issues are typically much less dramatic than the dramatic ones that we see in the major television and film productions that focus on the life of serial killers and other criminals. As we continue to take these types of relationships for granted as normal, the more difficult it becomes to spot these as problematic.

Keep in mind that psychological, emotional and social predators are not viewed as ill. The lack of morality or empathy and their ability to adapt from at an young age to adhere to the rules and practices which may be completely incorrect, could cause them to be a bit terrifying. But, it is important to keep in mind that while their arrogance as well as their lack of understanding might permit them to gain unfair advantages within relationships, the mental abilities stem from insufficient development and not an advanced evolutionary state.

Chapter 3: Dark Psychology Strategies

Psychopaths as well as sociopaths and other who engage in dark psychological practices are able to stay in the shadows is that at first glance they appear to be delightful, friendly individuals. They are aware of how to be friendly and what charm they can be able to use to manipulate people to their wishes. While doing this, they are attempting to detect signals from body language, facial expressions, words used by people and even their appearance. The information they gather can be used to manipulate people who surround them. This chapter will go over the most well-known techniques of dark psychology, such as manipulating the mind, using persuasion techniques deceit, covert neuro-linguistic programming along with emotional manipulation.

Mind Manipulation

People love to get their ways. Even if they don't intend to manipulate They can be so obsessed with their goals that they adopt an 'ends justify the approach to their actions. That means they're willing to use manipulation and even commit crimes to get what they need. Here's a look at a few of the most popular manipulative strategies you might come across:

* Semantic Manipulation - People who employ this technique manipulate words. They employ words with the same meaning that is generally accepted and then claim that they had a different interpretation regarding the topic. For instance, someone who you're casually dating could claim that they really like you as a way to indicate their desire to pursue things. If you do not like them, they could claim that it wasn't what they intended and they really do appreciate you as a person. They may have changed their words to avoid feeling rejection.

* Reverse Psychology This method involves telling someone a specific thing to motivate them to act in the opposite direction. Imagine, for instance, that a sister doesn't have her brother a present for his birthday yet because it's his birthday. Her father claims that her absence of a gift is due to her being poor, stingy and doesn't care about her brother. To show him that she is not she buys a more expensive present.

* Home Court Advantage - It's awkward and intimidating to reach someone's number when you're at their home or office. If manipulators are able to invite you into their private spaces they're making use of the venue for meeting. It is normal for people to feel more scared when they are in unfamiliar areas. Because they own the territory and are familiarity, they are at an advantage over you and could utilize this to influence.

* Negative Surprises- If you're caught by surprise you are less likely to consider your

options prior to when you have to provide an answer. For example, someone who works for a publication might hire an unexperienced writer to write an article. As the deadline approaches the writer is told that they require an extension or the publication won't be able to print the article in any way. They present it like it doesn't matter what they decide, but they must make an answer soon in order for the company to keep working with them. The editor of the magazine may grant an extension, but only because they're put on the spot just prior to the deadline, and they are unable to come up with a contingency plan.

Dark Persuasion

Persuasion is a vital capability to possess when you need to convince someone to accept your views. It is crucial in the workplace when you have an opinion that is different from yours as well as when you're introducing new concepts. This is why instructors assign persuasive writing assignments, because the ability to clearly and calmly present your argument to someone is crucial in influencing ethically. In the case of dark psychology, convincing someone could be done by manipulative methods such as the following:

* Invoking AuthorityAbusing Authority Authority is among the most effective ways to persuade anyone to do something. Someone who is trying to convince you using dark psychology may use an official source or inform you that they have read an article on the subject to support their argument. In certain cases, the source or article might be completely untrue. They are betting that you will not follow up on their sources and following the advice they've asked for.

* Twisting Information is not unusual that dark psychology experts alter information in a manner which supports their theory. It is a good idea to convince someone to believe something by giving details, it's the method they use to alter it that is

detrimental. For instance, they could make you feel uncomfortable by declaring that someone was speaking about you but failing to inform that the person was making a statement about the other person in a constructive manner and insisting that it is your responsibility to meet with them.

* Asking for Less - A popular method of persuasion is to solicit less. The dark psychologist may solicit something that you will not offer them, like a loan of $500. If you do not agree to the request, they'll request $80 for something (to pay one of their expenses). They will insist that even that little amount can be a big difference. Because you've already rejected their request in the first instance and you're now obliged to loan them the less amount. Hurrying Your Decision People who make decisions quickly will almost always try to conceal some thing. For instance the wife may visit a dealership for cars and the salesperson may try to convince her to

purchase a substandard vehicle. If she tells him that she'll be back on the following day, with husband in to inspect the vehicle once more and the salesperson may try to convince her to buy the car. He may offer a price reduction or mention that there's an other person who is interested. Anything to stop her from taking the time to conduct further research and determine if the vehicle is not safe.

* Do not speak firstLet someone else take the chance to speak first is not always a good idea. Sometimes, it's the person who is looking for an opportunity to discover your weaknesses and take advantage of them. It's not unusual for manipulators to pose questions. When you respond your questions, you're providing an outline that they can utilize to analyse your emotions, thoughts, and actions. They can then utilize the information they gather to influence your behavior in the future.

* Overwhelming by FactsImagine it's Friday and you have 10 minutes prior to calling to end your night. A supervisor comes over and places a huge pile of papers on your desk. He is insisting that you get them to be signed prior to your departure. There's no way to go all the documents prior to the time you have to go home, so you take a few hours or sign the documents without doing any reading. When manipulators desire to do something, they could overpower a person with information. They can't filter through the vast amount of information and are therefore more likely to follow whatever the dark psychology is looking for.

* Playing dumb- even when dark psychologists may think they are more superior than the other people around them, this should not mean they cannot pretend they're not aware of some thing to make someone bend to their wishes. For example, a worker could go into work late at night and work tasks. If they are

arrested in the following day, the boss is stern with them. They inform their bosses that they didn't know the rules, and thus get free of the shackles. Dark psychologists can also fake ignorance to convince people to help them. For instance, a coworker may come up to you and say they do not know what they need to know to present. They want you to help with the organization and then put it together. If you're willing to help they might even contact you later, with an excuse that they're unable to assist but insisting that you complete the task. completed.

Fraud

Dark psychology practitioners are deceiving in various ways. The attractive, charismatic facade they present in order to lure someone in is false since it's not their real persona. It is also a matter of convincing someone of their opinions. Even if they don't commit a blatant lie, psychopaths can exaggerate, conceal lies, or avoid the disclosure of important details. Although the average person might be honest and not feel vindictive People who are psychopaths can consistently lie without plausible motive. One example is when a friend fails to let you know that your ex is at a gathering because they know that you don't be able to attend when they're at the party.

Choice restriction is another technique that dark psychologists make use of deception. They make someone make a an unpopular choice on the basis of limited choices. There are occasions that this isn't necessarily an issue but it can be manipulative. One is then made to pick something the psychopath wants since they only have certain choices. For instance, a mom may ask her child to choose between macaroni or chicken nuggets, or even chicken nuggets and cheese to eat for dinner. This allows them to assert their independence and avoid the annoyance of your toddler crying when mom tells them they can't enjoy the ice cream that they requested.

Covert Neuro-Linguistic Programming

It takes years of study to master. It's an investigation of brain function and how specific events trigger a response. Imagine that two people are shown a photo of a snake. For one of them the snake causes an anxiety reaction. There are a variety of snakes that are deadly within the region in which they reside, and they're afraid of the possibility of getting bitten. For some this same image of a snake may cause feelings of happiness or satisfaction. People might be thrilled to look at the snake since they consider it to be an interesting creature or as a toy.

Neuro-linguistic programming started as the study of human performance. A specialist in language and IT scientist collaborated in the University of California in the 1970s. They studied the results of those with similar backgrounds, training, education and experiences. They discovered that despite the fact that all of these variables were the same, people scored on different levels in assessing their superiority. Based on studies, it was concluded that the inner workings of a person are more important to their performance or inability to achieve it, not their education or background. Things like experience in life as well as self-image, attitude and influence the way your mind works with words and the way it reacts to specific words.

Dark psychologists employ neuro-linguistic programming successfully because they are able to detect people. They can gather information about your thoughts throughout time, using simple conversations, and also by watching your body language and facial expressions. signals when they speak certain words. They also analyze how your eyes move to determine how you use the information within your brain. Most people do not know how much they're giving away by the physical posture of their bodies and the tiny facial expressions they display.

Traditional neuro-linguistic programming typically involves the therapist working with the patient to assist them in reaching the desired result, usually the outcome is some kind of successful outcome. Dark psychologists employ the more obscure version of NLP. They gather clues about the internal workings of your brain over time since answering too many of the questions can cause them to become suspicious. Once they have accumulated sufficient information, they can modify their words and behavior in a manner that encourages you to offer them what they need. In the event that the dark psychologist becomes intimate with the victims hidden neuro-linguistic programming could be a means that controls your mind.

Emotional Influence

Sometimes, they take advantage of your emotions in order to profit from your vulnerability. People are usually emotional. Although you may react to the things around you but it is your emotion that causes the behaviour. Here are some of the ways people manipulate your emotions in order to get their ways:

* Love Denial - This is a manipulative tactic that is used to squelch affection. For instance women might not want to cuddle her husband because she saw him looking at the waitress during their date.

* Love Flooding: This can also be referred to as buttering an individual up.' It's making use of affection or compliments to get someone to be more relaxed prior to asking them for something. For instance, a friend may notice that you are adept in building things and request for help in building the deck.

* Withdrawal is one of the strategies that is referred to as "the silence treatment. While withdrawal is useful to help someone relax and let them process their emotions, this strategy is a form of

punishment to the person who is being punished. For example, a friend may not answer their phone for a couple of days after they observe them texting with the person they love at a gathering.

* Emotional blackmail- Emotional blackmail is available in many forms. One of the most common strategies is guilting that is designed in order to cause someone else to feel guilty because they made a choice that is against the wishes of the manipulator. Dark psychologists can also use criticism and judgement to lower the self-esteem of a person, particularly one they're in the same relationship. If the person tries to break up with them, they could claim that they will never be able to find someone who loves them back or tell them that they're not enough to be loved. It is not unusual for manipulators to threaten to hurt themselves or use threats to provoke fear. This is a deterrent strategy.

"Playing The Victim" playing the victim is a game which is used to call the sympathy of other people. For instance, a colleague might say their child is sick and must go to the emergency room making it their justification for throwing their work on someone else. It is possible that they do this regardless of regardless of whether their child has a medical condition or not. They know the other coworkers will think that it was insensitive to ask whether they're lying. Psychologists who are dark may employ this method if you point them on their manipulative behavior. They could share a painful tale of their early years or relationships that was constantly manipulative, while insisting that they had no idea that they were manipulating.

Through some of the methods that are discussed in this chapter there are many ways to be utilized ethically. For instance, it's moral for a mom to offer her child two options to prevent an argument. It's also acceptable to employ techniques like reverse-psychology or similar methods in certain situations. Remember that the ends don't always justify the methods. If you don't want to be willing to share your work with someone else, the chances are that you're using methods that are not ethical to employ. Be aware that the information you find in this article is intended to protect you from mental assaults. It is not recommended to make use of the information to ruin the lives of others.

Chapter 4: Art of Persuasion

We're getting into more detail about how you can utilize psychology to support your personal growth and help you to advance in your life by utilizing the most ethical methods. The first method that is psychologically sound that can not only aid in that direction but also protect you from manipulators and dark psychology users is the art of persuasion.

Persuasion is the method of influencing people to perceive things in the same way you want them to behave in a specific way that is beneficial to both sides. Simply saying something to someone and then having them perform it is not convincing. One example is to tell a child that they must go to bed at a particular time each night. While the child may follow through due to their respect of a guardian or parent's authority but the child hasn't been persuaded to go sleep that hour. In the absence of the parent's exercise of authority and authority, the child will not be able to sleep at the time. The child's belief that time of bed is in his or her best interest has not changed.

Also, following the instructions of a boss or doing something that is required by a professor does not constitute persuasion. The purchase of a product that is brand-name in the event of a sale is not considered persuasion, as the purchaser will return to usual buying habits once prices rise to normal.

None of the scenarios described above can be considered persuading since the person who performs the act hasn't changed the way they think because of the influence of an authoritative group.

Persuasion is the process of convincing someone to behave in a specific manner due to a change in beliefs. Thus, persuasion occurs when there is a shift in attitude and action.

The idea of persuasion can be simple: get others to believe in the same thing you do, and then follow through with that conviction. The method isn't easy however. The difficulty lies in the fact that one must tap into the beliefs of another to change their mindset that will lead to the action. There is a method for learning how to persuade which anybody can learn and use. These methods will be explained in the following paragraphs.

Is Persuasion ethical?
Persuasion isn't manipulation. The intention behind manipulative tactics is to force an individual to do something that isn't beneficial to them. Persuasion on the contrary, is a method of persuading people to perform actions which are not beneficial to them but also to the interest of the persuader.

As with all other forms that art can use, convincing by itself is not good or harmful. The issue of morality or morality arises because of the way it is utilized. If someone uses persuasion in order to manipulate or harm others, then , of course, that person is using persuasion in a way that is considered unmoral. There are, naturally many instances when persuasion's technique was employed in an unethical manner. In these cases the persuader focused on their own needs and did not consider the interests of others. One of the fundamentals of persuasion (discussed further below) can be that the individual who is being persuaded should benefit or gain by being convinced, if the persuasion is conducted in an ethically acceptable manner.

A person who is using dark psychology does not follow this rule and may even commit an act of persuasion to act in a way which is detrimental to the individual. This is referred to as unjustified influence. It occurs when a dark psychologist or manipulator uses persuasion methods to convince a person to do something that is against their own decision or causes serious consequences for the person. A good example is a caretaker who convinces the incapacitated person to alter the conditions of their wishes to allow the caretaker to receive the entirety of their belongings. Based on this scenario you can observe that the influence is unjustified when the person being persuaded isn't in a position of mind to take decisions on their own.

Even though persuasion could be utilized in a negative manner however, there's a lot of good that comes from the practice. In fact, I would bet that if you don't master this art and be able to master it, one would struggle to lead the life they would like to live because the success in many fields is contingent upon our capacity to convince others to support us. It is unlikely that a person can be able to get the job they want when they are unable to convince the recruiters to accept the job. The person won't be married to the love of their life in the event that they fail to convince the other person to join them in holy marriage. Sometimes, a couple cannot purchase their dream house when they can't convince the loan officer of the bank to grant them an mortgage.

The art of persuasion can make more likely you'll be a victim of those who use persuasion to gain advantage. You're less susceptible to be deceived if you know who attempts to influence your decision-making. Of course, anyone trying to influence your decisions does not need to be interpreted in a malicious manner. But knowing that you can choose in the final analysis, to either say"yes" or "no," you are able to put yourself in powerful position.

Additionally, it reduces the possibility that you'll be misled, knowing that the persuasion can help enhance your social skills and helps build confidence in yourself as it boosts self-esteem. Persuasion is a skill that can be learned and aids in the management of mental health issues such as anxiety and depression.

The Basic Principles of Persuasion

Certain individuals are naturally persuasive, while it can take some effort for others to grasp it. However, no matter how easily one is able to practice the art of persuasion there are certain rules to be followed for persuasive methods to be efficient but also ethical. We'll take a closer look at each of these fundamentals upon that the practice of moral persuasion is based below.

Reciprocation

The primary principle is reciprocation, because it's founded on the idea that when you show kindness to people, they feel the need to repay the favor, regardless of any pressure from you. If, for instance, someone gives that is a birthday present and you are compelled to repay the gift and gift that person something to celebrate their birthday. If you're invited out by an acquaintance, you have the responsibility of inviting your friend next time you plan to go out to a place which is important to the person. The reciprocation principle can even be extended to social media in the present day and time. If someone shares and likes your article on Facebook You will probably want to replicate the same process whenever they share a post.

It is believed that this is a result of the evolution of humans, which was developed to aid each other to survive in the wilderness. In your persuasion strategy, begin by making small gestures to help others. It is a good habit to give these gestures to people within your family, community and at work. People often feel people are offering gestures of appreciation to receive something in return. Therefore, it should be part of your routine to show kindness to people around you. This can be accomplished by volunteering, taking part in charitable events or finding the right cause to support.

When you do this you establish a name of being a good person to others. It's a quick process and all that the person who needs your persuasive efforts is do a little research to determine if your previous actions are indicative of your natural ability to give. It makes you appear to be a trusted person in people's eyes , and consequently your influence is broader. This makes persuasion much simpler.

Aside from that I'd like to mention that helping your community can bring wonderful feelings of meaning and fulfillment in a person's life. It is a wonderful method to not just expand your influence circle but to also find the purpose of your life.

Engagement

The person you are trying to persuasion to make a verbal commitment to follow through with the actions you like to see happen makes it more likely that the follow-through will be accomplished. Without an agreement to an action plan by the conclusion of an interaction, the individual is more likely not to take action since they do not have committed to doing so. There is usually an internal urge that prompts them to take the action they have previously signed off on. Additionally, they feel they're more reliable when they perform the actions they've committed to. These two factors are more likely to ensure that the method of persuasion will succeed.

Authority

It is a very powerful concept that can be applied to persuasion. However, with its power comes a variety of risk when it is used by manipulators and users of dark psychology. People are inclined to take extreme measures to satisfy people they think are being in a position of authority over them. For instance, many people are not able to doubt the actions their doctor has recommended. If that doctor has someone with a dark character it is impossible to know what harm someone could create for themselves through their desire to obey someone who they believe has the authority to control their actions.

A lot of people wearing uniforms like nurses and policemen are viewed as being in a position of authority and , therefore their influence over other people is more powerful. This can be used to your advantage, but in an ethical way.

Even without uniforms an individual who does typically assertive in their manner may appear to have authority and , therefore, become more persuasive.

Social Validation

In general the public is more likely to be convinced after seeing evidence that the idea has worked well for others. When trying to convince others to believe in your idea, make sure that you have collected social proof that your concept has improved the lives of others by generating value. We see evidence of this daily through social media. Public profiles and companies with large followers are more likely to influence others to join the following and try out products when they are offered for sale.

Scarcity

Value is a scale of relative value. What one person may perceive as extremely valuable may be viewed as having an unimportant worth to another. For instance, one individual may see a gold necklace as a valuable item when compared to connecting with family members and a different person may see social connections as more valuable than possessions such as the gold chain. Whatever someone believes is important, the value is generally interpreted by the items that others would like.

I'm sure you've heard that people are looking for things they can't have, and if you're the one to provide the thing that is in short supply and therefore, convincing is made easier. For instance, a person who sees that a gold chain is superior to interpersonal connections might not have access to the materials like those. It is a scarce item in the person's lifetime and thus it is most likely they are able to buy if the money are readily accessible.

On the other hand people who view interpersonal relationships as more valuable could be more difficult to build these connections, or perhaps experienced an event which convinced them that relationships are worth more than possessions. Your task as the persuasive person is to help your client realise that the thing you desire is not easily accessible and thus important. The more value you can bring to the table even if it's by yourself more likely you are to convince others to believe that the idea you're trying to convey to them is important.

Likeability

Being loved is an excellent influencer, as it reflects an individual's trustworthiness. It is logical that people who are not trustworthy have shown signs of fraud and therefore, aren't liked by a large portion of the population. However, if an individual is trustworthy you are likely to see them admired by the general public. If you are a fan of someone or have a relationship established, it's more likely that you'll agree with their argument.

Being popular is not a requirement that you have to always be a good listener. It just means that you must develop the ability to be diplomatic and respect the way you interact with others. Likeability is a major influencing element in races that depend on the opinions of other people like presidential elections.

Chapter 5: Deceit Beyond the Little White Lie

Everyone has done it. Little children aren't sure who did the dirty work or damaged the lamp. The check is now in the mail. We'll be in the office in five minutes. Yes, you look stunning in the dress. The little white lies. It's part of the human nature. Before we examine the ways we can make use of deceit and deceit we should look at the reasons we lie.

Lies!

If we are wired to lie, what is the reason? Where does the urge to lie originate? Does it come from a biological or psychological source or both? It's both! Humans are prone to lying due to the scientific term "tend and defend" reaction. It means that lying is utilized to satisfy requirements or to defend against threats, and there is a connection with lying, and the release of chemical in our brains called oxytocin. It is one of our instinctual "feel good" hormones. If we experience an elevated level of oxytocin we tend to lie more often in order to keep that feeling of a natural buzz.

There are many plausible reasons for lying that fall under either the defense or tend category. They can be described as follows:

1. Protect oneself from harmThis is a lie that is designed to avoid repercussions or punishment for actions or perceived actions;

2. Defend other people2. Lie to others in order to prevent others from being criticized or punished for their perceived or actual actions.

3. Tend to selfThese are lies that are told to control an individual or situation and to avoid embarrassment and uncomfortable social circumstances, that are told to fulfill personal desires or gain admiration.

Four Tend to OthersTell lies to guard the secrets of others in order to build others to be more powerful than they really are and to keep up public appearances.

They don't need to be life-changing however, when they get too extensive, it becomes difficult to keep a tale in order. The best lies contain a bit of truth, and it appears to be the situation. Falsehoods can have severe consequences after they are exposed If you're planning to deceive people make sure you are emotionally ready to handle any consequences.

The repercussions of Pinocchio's lies was manifested physically in an expanding nose!

What is the point at which lies turn into deceit?

If you contemplate lies, then you'll find that they're on an equivalent scale. A simple white lying about having no babysitter may keep you from attending a party, therefore, it's not too high in the rest of them. If you tell the truth that you don't have a babysitter however, you don't really need one since you lie about having a child this is a bit of a big deal. What's the right limit?

Little lies, or fibs are usually not accompanied by any consequences. However, bigger lies, specifically those that are compounded by repetition or adding, result in a cycle of lying that ultimately is destructive to others, self, or even self. The cycle of lying is the final line that separates lying and deceit.

The deceit can take different forms- lying about your work or life experiences and lying about the condition of relationships you have, deceitful acts of omission, or even lies that are repeated repeatedly, and the people who lie are convinced. If lying can cause so many psychological harms and psychological harm, why do we continue to use these types of lies?

How do they apply in real Life

It's the same as the "tend or defend" response. Let's take a deeper review of the reasons why people might employ lies to achieve these goals. The primary reason that came up was to defend oneself. Self-defense is an effective factor. If you're in a toxic relationship You may be lying about the place you've been in order to protect yourself from being attacked physically or verbally even though your place of residence is a place that's safe in a relationship that is healthy. If the person who is threatening you thinks that you went to the grocery store instead of enjoying coffee with a buddy and you've made up a lie to shield yourself from being abused.

The third reason was to defend other people. This could be a similar scenario as described above, but maybe it's a mom lying to shield her children from being emotional or physically abuser of authority. A different scenario could be an older sibling assuming the responsibility for their behavior but it was actually the younger sibling who caused damage or damaged an item of value. Coworkers or friends may pretend to stand up for one another in instances they would otherwise be caught in the crossfire.

The next thing to be mentioned about the reasons people lie is because they tend to themselves. There are many reasons to lie, and this is probably the most prevalent motive as well. People lie to satisfy their personal needs and wants to gain what they desire from others. People lie to get others to admire them. Therefore, they embellish their personal achievements and accomplishments to make themselves appear better. We see this happen in the case of the fraudulent use of a resume or transcript.

People who tell lies to look after themselves often are discussed, not intentionally however, with the intention to cover any embarrassing circumstance or to avoid awkward social encounter. They could be used to conceal a mistake or even to avoid a gathering you're not going to. Although these aren't big falsehoods, you could get a bit of backlash if your husband's irritating cousin discovers that you're not really sick to go to her bridal shower, which is just two hours away.

The final type of deceit is that people tell in order to be nice to other people. It can be a matter of lying about how much they like someone's haircut, or telling lies about how great one is at their job in order to provide them with an accurate reference. Telling lies to other people are more likely to be of a positive character however this doesn't mean they're not vulnerable for the negative effects like other kinds of lies.

Famous Deceptions and Cases

Deception is among the most popular methods used in dark psychology. Deception is used throughout the course of human historical. In the case of Trojan Horse is a fabulous illustration that shows the effectiveness of tricks and deceit. The whole population believed that they received a present but was slain in the end.

In the current era one of the most significant stories that have emerged from the deceitful foundations has been the rise as well as demise of Elizabeth Holmes and her health technology company Theranos. Holmes claimed that she created a blood test machine that could make full diagnoses by using just a small amount of blood. This was done primarily using a fingerstick. Holmes made her board of directors totally fooled by her claims, and these weren't people who had a job.

The billionaire mogul of media Rupert Murdoch, the Walton family of Walmart fame, as well as The DeVos family, who founded Amway All fell victim to Holmes's deceit when they became investors of her biotech company. Holmes even fooled a number of well-off and educated board members including a number of former or the future United States Presidential Cabinet members. Holmes's deck of cards came in a crash when it was discovered that her nifty blood testing device was flawed and may even have endangered the health of those who depended on it. Before her deceit was revealed, Holmes had managed to amass an net value that was $4.5 billion, the entirety of which has disappeared today.

Holmes has a way of fooling several of the most famous business and scientific names across the nation and around the world. That's some serious deceit!

It is the Art of Crafting a Good Truth

Selling lying are two totally distinct things. Everybody knows when a child lies regarding who was the one who painted his wall in their living room. When it's time to deceive How do you come up with an enticing story that's plausible and waterproof?

In order to tell a convincing lie the lie must be at least partially based on the truth. It's much more easy to keep in mind, and you'll be able to offer an argument that you have only did what you could, and not lying in case you're discovered. Also, you should create your lie as easy as possible, in order to be able to use fewer details that could make a mistake. If you're in a position to devise your own deceit try telling it in a few practice sessions. It will emerge much more naturally when you are ready to reveal it.

Don't attempt to involve others in your lies. The more people that know about the truth, the better chances of being discovered. The truth and the secrets should be kept to you. It is best to keep the conversation short and use your usual manner when you tell your story. Your body eyes and language are consistent with your words, and ensure you are able to make yourself believe what you're trying to convey.

After you've confessed your lies Remove any evidence. If you made a social media post, delete it. If you've written something down, ensure that you delete the paper. The most important thing is to not amplify the lie by committing another. If you are arrested, it's likely better to just confess. Why? Because if you're honest and are truthful You're less likely to be caught the next time around.

Pants on Fire

Wouldn't you love it to actually find someone lying due to their pants going up in flames? But, liars, liars and burning pants isn't an actual thing. There are methods for determining whether someone is lying, and there are no flames. Pay attention to the eyes of someone when they are speaking to you. If they don't seem to be able to keep eye contact with you or seem to be very fidgety, they may not be honest about their feelings.

The ability to recognize the lie is more than the fidgeting and shifting eyes, but. If someone is experiencing an interruption in their speech or displays a pause in their behavior that doesn't usually occur or display, they could be in fact lying. According to some experts, an indicator of lying is when people who don't usually touch their mouth or face is doing so when speaking. also, when they play with or run the fingers of their head.

Speech signals can also indicate the possibility of someone in fact lying. If someone asks you very basic questions and then doesn't answer it could mean they are making use of time to create an untrue answer. Be aware of any insufficient details when asked an unintentional question. If you believe you've been deceived you, ask the person you're talking to to repeat their story and in reverse. The capacity for cognitive processing to recall a lie can lead them to fall when they have to relay it out of the order.

Although there's no 100% sure method of determining whether someone is lying to you, follow these suggestions and follow your gut. You'll discover that you'll increase your chances of identifying an untruthful person. Do not dismiss your intuition They can reveal much more about body language or conversation patterns could ever tell you.

Chapter 6: What is the Dark Triad?

Certain people possess personality characteristics that make them difficult or even impossible to work with these individuals. They could be volatile and arrogant or domineering However under the right management you can help them develop their strengths, eliminate the negative aspects of their behaviour and restore harmony in the team.

Certain other actions or traits could be detrimental and, if one exhibits a negative combination of these traits, they may undermine his coworkers in a long-lasting way and could even ruin an entire team.

The Dark Triad is a phrase you're likely to hear in the workplace, however it's one of the most popular buzzwords in the world of psychology.

The Dark Triad is basically the description as the most harmful psychological characteristics that an individual could have. It is believed that the Dark Triad is just like the source from which all other kind of dark psychology originates. The three damaging traits include Narcissism, Psychopathy, and Machiavellianism.

Narcissism

Narcissism is a term that comes from the Greek mythology of Narcissus the hunter who became infatuated with his reflection the water in a pool and ended up drowning. Narcissistic individuals can be self-centered confident, boastful, arrogant without empathy and apathetic to criticism.

In general, people believe that it is self-love that is excessively strong. Narcissists are considered to be one with an over inflated self-esteem that sees oneself as superior to others. But, in essence it is possible to feel self-love and not be a narcissist. Someone who is able to meet the medical requirements for diagnosing narcissism up at a point where they are diagnosed with psychological disorders often displays characteristics associated with those who belong to the Dark Triad. The mental state of a narcissist can be so dark that they see himself as the highest form of human being, and that other people are designed only to help him. Their actions usually reflect the self-worth they have. A narcissist is not willing to be tolerant of criticism or accept that someone has opinions that differ from their own. Instead, they prefer to be applauded or even praised. They are enticed to be honored and always given praise and praise, and they are constantly striving to keep this standards.

Psychopathy

Psychopathic traits that are characteristic of a person include the lack of empathy, regret, antisocial behavior and being unpredictable and manipulative. It is important to recognize that there's a difference between psychopathic characteristics as well as being considered a psychopath and its affluence with violence committed by criminals.

A psychopath has a psychological illness that is characterized by superficial appeal, impulsivity and the absence of emotions such as remorse and empathy. Psychopaths don't feel any sympathy for other people and does not have any feelings of guilt for any wrongdoings they might have done. They live in their personal universe where the difference between right and wrong is determined by them and only themselves. So what a psychopath views as the normal and acceptable thing can be seen as unacceptable by others. Psychopaths are among the most dangerous individuals around and are sheep dressed as wolves. Some psychopaths appear to be as rational as other human beings, however their level of sanity is quite different from that of the average person's. The psychopaths who are truly dangerous to the world will likely be charming and attractive strangers who lure their victims' trust by engaging in the most loving ways , but ultimately damaging the lives of their victims They may even kill their victims as is usually the situation.

Many of the most well-known business names are psychopathic; for psychopaths have been known to rise to the top of the area they pick which is the top of the line and, once they reach this height, there's almost always nothing they can't do, and often they get out of their crimes. Psychopaths are enthralled by watching other people suffer and aren't bound by conscience or any remorse.

Machiavellianism

The word originates from the famous sixteenth Century Italian political and diplomatic figure Niccolo Machiavelli. The man gained notoriety through his book of 1513, "The Prince", was perceived as a reaffirmation of the dark art of deceit and cunning in diplomatic espionage. Machiavellianism's flaws include manipulation, duplicity of self-interest, as well as an absence of morality and emotion.

The source of this name can be traced back to that of philosopher Machiavelli. Machiavellianism is the determination to be focused on self-interest always and the need to be the first to take care of yourself above others. It is sometimes referred to as being selfish, but it's an actual thing. Machiavellianism is a brutal exercise of cruelty and the power it has over compassion and mercy. Machiavellianism folks are extremely intelligent They are extremely strategically minded in their life choices, and when something or someone is not up to their standard of expectation in terms of strategy they will dismiss that individual or thing, without any thought to the harm the actions of their deeds could cause the people they hurt. The most skilled Machiavellianismians aren't publically brutal in their actions but rather, they use a method of stealth. They are savvy enough to make decisions that serve their own needs and still maintain an image of goodwill to the public. This is why it's difficult to distinguish the true Machiavellianism inclinations in them. They often find the perfect justification for every step they've made. A former President Bill Clinton is an example of someone who exhibits Machiavellianism characteristics. He was involved in extra-marital affairs when in his office, and he was still loved regardless of his actions in contrast to other politicians who did the same and lost their careers by doing so.

The Use Of The Dark Triad

Narcissistic Acts

Many narcissists have fantasies of being admired and adored by a large number of people. as they get older they are inclined to strive to make those fantasies become reality, believing that being loved or revered is what they are meant to be. When they meet those who don't have the desire to praise them, they consider their actions to be an insult. They regard these uncompromising individuals as their most vile adversaries and will seek an opportunity to force them to submit to them or come up with a permanent solution for the cockroaches, by pressing on them with force.

The immense self-worth that narcissists feel in their inner world is typically reflected in their appearance and behavior. They are wired to have two distinct perceptions: the desire to be loved and loved by other people and the fear of rejection, criticism, or disapproval. It's the behavior of the narcissist to be followed. Being worshiped is as important in their lives as breathing air and their fear of criticism is as poisonous.

Psychoopathic Effects

Psychopaths can be difficult to recognize, except for experienced psychotherapists who are well-trained, as they look and behave like normal humans, like other people and their actions when they are in public can be viewed as acceptable and even worthy of imitation. If you take the time to study the visible but subtle signs of psychopathy displayed by those who exhibit it, you'll be able identify these individuals, or at the very least be able to suspect them of having psychopathic characteristics.

Being charming is an outward character trait of someone with psychotic characteristics. Charm is typically not the real and real one, but it's fake superficial. Psychopaths show all the visible indicators of charm, such as physical attractiveness, and an interest in others. They employ charm as a tool to draw their victims in. They are aware that people tend to be capable of being more relaxed around those who show attractive traits to them. Therefore, they behave in a manner that is charming toward their victims. Any charm that a psychopath displays is only planned and calculated and never innate. Psychopaths don't have the positive qualities of charm. rather, they carry it out in order to be likely to get them the desired result.

Lying is also one of the characteristics of the psychopath. The mere fact that someone lies does not mean that someone is a psychopath. However, when it's combined with other traits, it can be a psychopathic character. If a psychopath doesn't lie is not a psychopath. The ability to lie is among the most powerful tools that psychopaths can employ. It is as natural to psychopaths as breathing ; psychopaths are utterly liars, and they're so adept in the art and art of deceit that their victims are unable to discern that they're lying.

Psychopaths have no remorse. They are so driven by their drive to attain their goals that there is no limit to the line they're willing to cross. And when they cross the line, they are required to allow themselves to guilt. They keep their conscience within the depths of their minds , so that they don't feel any guilt or shame over the act, even if they get caught. Anyone who commits a crime like murder typically feels so deeply guilty that a few may resort to suicide to alleviate themselves of the guilt. However, this is not the case for psychopaths who are enthralled by their crime and wants to be more successful since they are fueled by the sense of guilt. For a psychopath to be ashamed of what they've done is similar to the blind man being asked to drive a car on a highway. Psychopaths do not feel guilt because the idea of morality and right and wrong is not a factor to them. What they believe is what is essential and what's not. What's beneficial or not; there is no restriction on what they could accomplish when they think it is beneficial. It is not important to them whether it's unjust, a sin, or criminal. The only way that a psychopath can be remorseful or guilty is if they are not able to fulfill their psychopathic desires at the level they would like, or get caught before they are competent to carry out the act. In this situation it is possible that they feel guilty as they may believe that they've failed themselves. The idea that a psychopath could be ashamed of what they've caused to other objects such as animals or humans is a bit absurd.

Control issues are another sign of a psychopath. In contrast to normal humans, psychopaths have control over certain actions. A husband whose wife is constantly pestering and cursing at him at home might be able to keep from assaulting his wife however that is not the case for psychopaths. If a psychopath believes it is essential to put her down then he will not hesitate for a second to perform the action. You can even slap her if it will stop the wife from complaining but he'll not hesitate or be hesitant in killing her completely when he intends to silence her to make her happy. Once he has done this, he won't be ashamed of his actions at all; rather it will be blissful the peace and tranquility that the death of his wife gives him and then go on to his own life without ever thinking about the impact of his own actions. That's how the mind of a psychopath works. Psychopaths recognize opportunities and seize these opportunities without a sign of hesitation. An opportunity could be killing someone they would like to kill, taking items they would like to steal, or raping people they would like to be raped by. It is this complete inability to resist that makes psychopaths extremely successful in the military because they are able to do their best in completing their the tasks assigned to them. In the business world as well, psychopaths can succeed due to the fierce instinct they possess. Lack of a necessary drive is detrimental to the progress of people on the path to success, whether they are psychopaths or not.

Psychopaths also aren't able to feel emotions such as empathy. Psychopaths are incapable of feeling sad or angry for people around them, particularly when they suffer. Instead of feeling sorry for their fellow sufferers, psychopaths are enthralled by the type of suffering they suffer and, if they had the chance to cause more harm to the person they will. Psychopaths love watching loss of life through the eyes of animals or humans. If a psychopath is aware of an unfortunate incident happen to another person, the first thought in their minds is thinking about what they can do to help their own or how might utilize the tragedy for gain their own selfish advantage. Anyone looking for a sense of humaneness or compassion from a psychopath does nothing more than pouring water into the basket and hoping for the basket to fill up to capacity in a short time. Psychopaths must be kept away from the world since the brains of psychopaths take pleasure in inflicting pain.

Machiavellian Actions

Machiavellian is a Machiavellian individual is politician or person who is focused on maintaining a positive image in the public eye even when their actions and choices aren't in harmony. They make people believe that they're worthy to be followed, and of being seen to be a model but their secret intentions are filled with infidelity. Because Machiavellian individuals are adept in concealing their behavior They are usually difficult to identify; even when identified for doing grave crimes, the public is unable to believe that they're capable of doing the things that they're accused of and consequently, they take their ire at the accusers who accuse them of being liars and people who want to get publicity. Even to this day the goodwill that was left by Michael Jackson still lives on even after his passing, given the number of allegations that had been made against his name. Instead of being snubbed by the general public because of the allegations made against an Machiavellian person They are admired more due to the allegations they've been able to provoke a feeling of pity from the public. These are just a few methods employed by proficient Machiavellian individuals. The public persona of the Machiavellian person is simply an idealized image of who they are inside, and if individuals could discern the truth behind the public image of false self-esteem, it's easy to recognize who they actually are. This kind of process however, is next to being impossible.

Machiavellian people are aware of who they really are as well as how others consider them. This is what makes them dangerous and possibly vulnerable to being discovered. They realize that they need to maintain their image in the eyes of others and there's no chance of them being exposed even if victimized by their own clients in the future. They know the psychological makeup of those who follow and hold them in a high position. Mass murderers have been able to get away with their crimes for years because their perception of them is completely opposite from what that a killer is supposed to be. Imagine a religious leader famous for their charitable activities and compassion for others when they commit horrendous crimes of sexual assault and violence in private. For a long time people would never accuse such people for anything because their public image of the persona hides their true selves from others. True Machiavellian people instill both fear and love within the minds of the people who follow them, however, they do it in that fear is not forced like love. It has been crafted inside the brain of the person who follows them to be afraid and to love the people who are the.

Sadism

While sadism is an idea distinct from Machiavellianism Psychopathy as well as Narcissism however, it has an important influence in the Dark Triad; this time it is referred to as the tetrad in which it is the 4th element Sadism is introduced to the three other elements. Sadism is among the most dark traits to comprehend because it's very difficult to identify with individuals who are well-known, particularly those in the general public.

Sadism is getting pleasure from others' sufferings. Sadists would prefer to watch a man suffer suffering than win the lottery. It's a really sick aspect of the dark side. For example when one Machiavellian person causes suffering of someone else They will not be able to regret it. Of course however that doesn't mean they'll enjoy the experience, however, when the person is also suffering from the sadism characteristic the person will get satisfaction from the pain that someone else is suffering and will eventually attempt to cause further suffering to the same person, or in other people in the same way. The thing that makes sadism so alarmingly distinctive is that the violence committed has nothing else to do with except satisfaction. A child with a sadistic streak will slice off a watermelon with brutality as he is trying to imagine the red interior of the fruit as flesh of a human. He'll take pleasure in believing that he has killed the human race. Sadists seek out the suffering of others because they are bored and need to entertain themselves. Some people spend huge sums of money to watch the victims of their actions.

Recognizing The Dark Triad Characteristics

The majority of psychologists discovered Dark Triad traits by measuring various personality types in isolation.

In 2010, however in 2010, the researcher Dr. Peter Jonason, then an assistant psychologist of the University of Western Florida, as well as his co-author Gregory Webster, assistant professor of psychology at the University of Florida, developed the "Dirty Dozen" rating scale, also known as an instrument that has 12 items, to assess Dark Triad traits.

Jonason Webster's measure and Jonason's ask individuals to assess themselves against these criteria:

I have a tendency to manipulate others to gain my desired results.

I've used deceit or used lies to get my way.

I have employed flattery to achieve my goals.

I am prone to exploit other people to gain my own advantage.

I'm prone to have no remorse.

I am not too focused on morality or ethicality of what I do.

I tend to be abrasive and insensitive.

I am a bit somewhat sarcastic.

I am prone to want people to be impressed by me.

I like to have others to pay attention to me.

I am prone to seeking fame or the status.

I usually expect certain favors from people.

At the most basic level the person will be evaluated from 1 to seven on any twelve tests giving a score of between 12 and 84. The greater the score, greater the likelihood of being diagnosed with Dark Triad tendencies.

Managing People With Dark Triad Traits

If you think an employee of your team exhibits Dark Triad personality traits, what do you do to address it? This is a thorny subject and there aren't simple solutions. Psychologists who have experience say that there are numerous subtleties and variations in personality types and behaviours associated with them could shift from day to day. However, as a leader you must tackle negative behaviors in order to maintain the harmony and efficiency of your team.

Spotting Manipulators

There are numerous methods to influence people. The power of praise and encouragement can encourage the team member to become more productive, as an example. However, if someone exhibits higher Machiavellian tendencies, they could attempt to influence colleagues by manipulating them for his own benefit, maybe by coercion or deceit.

The manipulative are usually adept in hiding their actions or actions, however there are some indicators you should be on the lookout for, for instance, people who refuse to take any kind of answer, or who will always justify her hurtful actions or presents an untrue "face" to various people in order to further her goals.

If you confront an untruthful person make sure you are specific about the behaviors you've observed and how they are affecting your team. Be clear about the fact that the behavior he is displaying needs to change, and think about an agreement to make him accountable.

Chapter 7: Manipulation Theories

Amplification Theory

In the course of my day-to-day job, I interact with many people. I've noticed something participating in discussions or forums. I observed that when people make statements frequently, and in a way that is credible, others began to believe in the information. I considered this, and then decided to conduct a bit of study. I eventually came across something called the theory of amplification. It is possible that if you make a statement with certainty and authority, your opinion becomes more solid and is spread to people around the world. This idea is especially relevant to the spreading of political views in the majority rule arena such as the internet. When people express their views by virtue of their power, other people will likely to agree with their views.

The Conversion Theory

A small group of suffragettes united in a passionate debate against the initially unpopular belief that women should be allowed to cast their vote. The tireless work of women's suffragettes, paired with their fairness eventually led the majority of the people to recognize their position.

Studies on similarity include a minor group who were adjusting to the dominant group. Moscovici contended along various lines. He claimed his belief that Asch (1951) and other had placed a great deal of emphasis on the idea that the dominant party at the gathering has an effect on the minorities. According to him that it is also possible for a minority to affect the majority of people.

In the end, Asch was in agreement with Moscovici. He also believed that the impact of minorities did occur and that it could be an issue that was becoming more crucial to consider in order to understand the reasons why some people might be influenced by minority sentiments and resist the growing pressure.

Moscovici distinguished between the two types of conversion and compliance. Conformity is commonplace in research, for instance Asch which is where members are free to follow the guidelines of the gathering but secretly reject them.

The conversion is about how minorities can influence an entire group. It involves convincing the majority part of the population that minority views are correct. This can be accomplished through diverse ways like the ability to be flexible, consistent and even. Conversion is different from consistency since its definition, in the vast majority of part, involves both open and private acknowledgement of a different opinion or behaviour.

How can the minority influence the views on the part of the majority?

Moscovici claims that a large part of impact willgenerally be based on open acceptance. This could be a case of uniformizing social impact. In this case, the impact of numbers is huge, but the the majority could compensate by expressing their support or even protest. In light of this, there's the pressure for minorities to make changes. Since the majority does not have a concern for minority's opinion about them the impact of minority groups is rarely built on the basis of regularizing social impact. It is instead based on the impact of education in offering the majority of people new perspectives or new information which causes them to think differently about their beliefs. In this context minorities' impact is the personal acknowledgment that changes more than a large portion of people by convincing people that the viewpoints of the minority are true.

Four main elements have been identified as important to a minority's ability to impact the majority.

These are known as social manner, style of reasoning as well as adaptability and evidence.

The Behavioral Style

This entails 4 segments:

Be consistent. The majority should be as consistent in the way they'd like to believe.

Be confident in the validity of their thoughts and the perspectives they're practicing

It gives the impression of being objective

Social weight and misuse

Moscovici added an idea that one of the important aspects of the behavior style is the consistency in the way people hold their positions. Constantly and consistently holding an opinion is more likely to affect the majority more than if a minority of people are discordant and changes their viewpoint.

Moscovici (1969) explored social styles (reliable/conflicting) on minority impact in his blue-green examinations. He showed that a stable minority was more efficient than a minority that was conflicting in changing perspectives of the greater part of.

Consistency could be important because:

When confronted with the same resistance people from the majority will stand up, listen, and then reevaluate their position.

Consistency creates the impression that the majority are convinced they are right and focussed on their viewpoint.

To alter the majority's opinion, the minority must offer a clear and unambiguous position, and should defend its position with a solid foundation.

A distinction can be created between two kinds of consistency:

The Diachronic Consistency is an ongoing consistency for a certain period of period of time. The majority of the time, its guns and doesn't alter its views.

The Synchronic Consistency is an underlying consistency between the individuals. In this case, all members agree and back each other up.

The Style of Thinking

Recognize three to four minority groups, such as refuge seekers, British National Party and others. What are your thoughts and how would you react to each one of these gatherings, and the viewpoints they bring for themselves? Do you dispel their views in all directions or contemplate what they should say and discuss their views with other people?

If you disapprove of the viewpoints of other people without considering the implications, you'd be spent your time thinking of shallow thoughts or preparing. However when you considered the viewpoints being argued then you would have been engaged with precise thinking and preparation. Research suggests that when a minority can bring the majority of the population to look at the issue and discuss arguments between them it, then the minority has a good chance of influencing the majority. If the minority can convince the majority to discuss and debate the arguments that they are making and advancing, the effect is likely more rooted.

Additionally, if the majority is rebuked by someone who has self-confidence and a determination to stand up for their beliefs and not defend their claim it is possible that the person in question may have a point.

Minority upsets that are reliable can be built up to standard and can make the situation unstable and conflicting. This could lead to the larger portion of the population to pay attention to what the views of minorities.

They will therefore have to be careful about their viewpoints.

Flexibility and Flexibility and

Different scientists have pondered whether the concept of consistency is sufficient for a minority to have an impact on the majority. They believe that the most important thing is how the majority of people perceive the meaning of.

If the true minority is considered to be a steadfast and rigid, solid and opinionated group and adamant, they are unlikely to alter the views of the majority. However If they appear flexible and willing to trade off with the majority, they will likely to be seen as less offensive, becoming more moderate, acceptable and sensible. In this way, they'll have a greater chance of changing the minds among the general public. Some researchers have advised that it's not only the existence of compromise and flexibility that is important but also compromise and flexibility.

The probability was analyzed in the work of Nemeth during 1986. The study was based on a fake jury in which the three jurors and one confederate were required to agree on the amount of money to be awarded to those who died in an accident on a ski lift. In the event that the majority of the group argued for a small amount and refused to change his view, he had no effect on the majority portion. If the bargaining process was completed and he shifted his way towards the larger that was in the majority, the majority was also affected and changed their position. This trial examines the importance of the consistency. The minority's position changed but it was not trustworthy, and the change that brought about the impact of minority groups.

Identification

People keep an eye on the persona of people that look similar to themselves. For example, men typically be more sociable with men, women with girls, children with other adolescents, and so on. Research has shown that when the majority is a minority group and they will be aware of the views on minority views and adjust their own views to match those of the minorities.

One study showed that a gay minority who fought for gay rights was less influential on a majority of straight people as opposed to a minority of straights arguing on behalf of gay rights. The majority of people who are not gay are associated with the minority of non-gays. They generally think of minorities that are not the same as them in that they are self-absorbed and anxious about the implications of advancing their particular reason.

Information Manipulation Theory

The theory is based on one of the four communicative maxims being purposefully broken by a person who is persuasive.

They are all four of them:

Quantity: This implies that the information you provide is complete and accurate. information.

Quality: Truthful and accurate information.

Communication is crucial.

Communication: The information is readily accessible and well-understood, non-verbal actions can help in determining the declaration's tone.

Priming

In the field of psychology , as well as manipulation of the mind it is a technique that involves presenting an enhancement affects the way people react to an improvement. Priming is a method of triggering an association or representation in memory before a subsequent improvement or task is introduced. This phenomenon happens in the absence of conscious awareness, yet it is able to significantly impact the various aspects of our day-to-day life.

What is the purpose of priming?

There are a variety of scenarios that demonstrate this function of priming can be used. For example, when you introduce someone with "yellow" will trigger an instant reaction in the mind of"banana

"banana" than to words that are not significant like "TV." Since banana and yellow are more strongly associated in memory, people react faster when the following word is spoken.

The preparation process can be aided by enhancements that can be connected in a variety of ways. For instance, the effects of priming occur perceptually in language, or conceptually related changes. The process of preparing can be a promising one with real applications in the field of learning and study aid, too.

Priming is the name given to a process to emphasize the significance of priming a water well. Once the well is made, the water will become created whenever it is switched on. When data has been stored in memory, it is likely to be reconstructed into consciousness more quickly.

Different types of priming

There are many distinct types of priming that can be found in the field of psychology and mind control. Every person has a specific objective in mind. They can be influenced by different ways.

Priming, both positive and negative show the impact of priming on the speed of handling. Priming with positives speeds up handling and speed up memory recovery while negative priming blocks it off.

Semantic priming is the use of words that are correlated to legally or etymologically. The first instance of reacting to "banana" to the extent that it does so quickly following being prepared using "yellow" is a sign using semantic primeing.

Acquainted preparation involves using two enhancements that are frequently linked. For example cat and mouse is a pair of words often linked in memory, and when one of them will trigger a reaction much faster when the next word comes up.

Reiteration priming occurs in the event that an update and reaction more than one time matched. This means that subjects are bound to react to a specific purpose in mind all the faster every time a boost is revealed.

Perceptual priming can be described as boosts that share similar structure. For example, "goat" will bring forth a faster reaction once it's gone than "boat" since both words are comparable.

Reasonable preparing involves the boost or reaction which are carefully connected. For instance, the words "work space" as well as "seat" are likely be able to demonstrate the impact of preparing because they're in the same category.

The masked priming consists of a part of the upgrade getting darkened or in another way, like by using hash marks. Although the entire upgrade isn't immediately apparent, nevertheless it triggers an emotional reaction. Words in which specific letters are obscured are a instance of priming that has been hidden.

The Priming Process

Therapists acknowledge that groups (or pattern) of information are stored into long-term memory. The process of triggering these patterns can be increased or decreased in various ways. As the beginning of particular elements of data is increased the recollections of these units become easier to reach. When activation decreases the data is found to be less likely to be retrieved from memory.

Priming is the process of determining which patterns are likely to begin as one. When you trigger a couple of pieces of data, other or related units also become dynamic. Why is it beneficial to have related compositions become more open and initiated? In a variety of scenarios having the ability to incorporate related data into memory quickly can help individuals in responding faster whenever the need arises.

For instance, the schemas associated with smooth roads and rainstorms could be closely linked in the memory. As you notice that the rain is descending, memories of possible smooth streets could ring a bell. Because your brain is trained to consider this information, you might be more prepared to react swiftly when you encounter an icy, wet section of road during your journey to home from work.

Genuine Impact

Priming has been observed in various courses in brain research . about labs. But, what impact does it affect the real world?

Training can influence how you See the world

The viral phenomenon that is Yanny as well as Laurel is an example of how preparation can affect how you perceive information. A sound sample that was ambiguous was sent by an online customer using a survey to find out the participants what they were hearing. A few individuals specifically were able to hear "Yanny," while others were able to hear "Tree." A few people even mentioned having the option of switching between or from the phrases they heard.

Due to the uncertainty of aural perception Clinical psychologists suggest that people use priming sounds to determine the sounds they will hear. The study suggests that we aren't able to hear through the breakdown of the frequencies of the noises that reach our ears before making decisions about the words the frequencies form. Instead, we employ what's known as the top-down method of handling. Our brains initially detect some sounds as being part of a discourse. After that our brains use settings to discern the meaning of these sounds.

This could help explain why people frequently confuse melodies and verses. If the melody is not clear your brain helps fill in the gap extremely and efficiently. The effects of priming would be able to turn into the most significant element. If you're prepared to understand a verse with a particular goal in mind, you'll likely to be able to understand it with a specific purpose in mind based on the primeing.

When it comes to hearing Yanny or Laurel Simply observing the concept of the sound clasp will make you be able to hear either the two. The way in which people who saw the video were then looking forward to hearing one of Yanny or Laurel made them hear both of these words, not just another word.

To explain this, the variables related to sound quality and hearing capacity played an additional part. Younger people with hearing loss that is not as old would have been more likely hearing "Yanny" due to the fact that their ears are more able to recognize sounds with higher frequency. The people who were able to hear Laurel was watching hearing sounds that were less frequent.

It can have an impact on your behavior in many ways

In one test, scientists were able to prepare participants for tests using words that are typically associated with stereotypes of older people. When they left the testing stall those who were taught words that were associated as being more experienced adults were likely to walk more slowly than those who were not trained.

A study published in the journal Aging and Mental Health found that preparing individuals that had negative mature generalizations had gradually negative effects on their practice and self-appraised assessment. The preparation of members with negative maturing generalizations resulted in an increase in feelings of despair and a greater frequency of helping-seeking.

The inference of generalizations about older people having a feeling of desperation, and loneliness caused people to feel more lonely and becoming more vulnerable. Researchers believe that exposure to these generalizations about age may cause increased reliance, and less self-assessments of capability and working capacity in older people.

Priming is also useful as a tool for education

Academicians and instructors can also make use of priming as an instructional instrument. Some students do better when they are aware of the things they are likely to encounter. Learning new information can be a challenge be a bit intimidating, but making sure that students are prepared by showing information prior to an exercise being provided can be helpful.

Priming is frequently used as a method of instructive mediation for students who have certain abilities in learning. It introduces new content prior to the time it is taught, allowing the student to be comfortable with it. For instance, students might be allowed to "review" the texts or other materials to be used in an exercise. As they're now familiar with the information and resources and are more prepared to concentrate when they are actually working.

Reciprocity Normal

The concept of reciprocity, is mentioned here and there as the standard of reciprocity is a social norm that states that the moment someone accomplishes something for you and you are gratified, you are compelled to repay them in a similar manner. One place where this concept is often used is the field of marketing. Advertisers employ a variety of strategies to convince consumers to buy. Certain are obvious such as coupons, discounts and other unusual developments. Certain are unmistakably less pretentious and rely on the human brain , a science that many people aren't at all aware.

This is the way it is. Have you ever had the feeling of being obligated to complete something for someone else because they've previously completed some thing for you? The quality of correspondence is just one type of social norm which can affect our conduct. The reciprocity standard is based with a basic rule: We'll generally, be committed to return support to those who give us favors. When your new neighbors offer some treats for you to enjoy in the area, you might be enticed to help them in manner.

Reciprocity in real life

A salesperson offering a free present to a prospective client hoping that it will inspire them to return the favor in the form of a purchase

A pioneer that offers assistance and support to supporters in exchange for their trust

Giving clients important information to help them pursue further marketing opportunities

This kind of behavior has a number of obvious benefits. When it comes to a particular thing it is beneficial to help others and increase the longevity for the entire species. When we respond, we can ensure that others receive help whenever they require it, and we receive assistance when we need it.

Reciprocity can also help individuals accomplish things they would not be able to accomplish on their own. Through cooperation or trading with administrations, individuals are able to accomplish greater results than they could by working alone.

Chapter 8: What is Emotional Manipulation?

The primary goal of manipulating your emotions is to cause you to lose control over your emotions. This will cause you to feel overwhelmed by emotions, while at the same time makes you more vulnerable. The advantage will be taken and they'll be able to access you and take what they'd like from you. To ensure that you're away from the wheel with your emotions, manipulators take you to a location that they are aware of as unfamiliar to you, but is they are familiar with. It will cause you to fall off your feet, but the new surroundings gives them the feeling of dominance and having control. You're new to the area and the manipulator is able to benefit from the space between the ability to adapt and regain control.

What Can An Emotional Manipulator Do?

They can undermine your faith in your ability to comprehend the truth.

They are extremely skilled lying liars. We say that an accident didn't happen because it happened, and even though we did nothing however, they claim that they did or said something. The issue is that they're so amazing at it that you are forced to reconsider your own health. The belief that the cause of the question was an act of the subconscious is an extremely powerful solution to difficulties.

Their actions are not in The Spirit of Their Terms

They can tell that you're in the right place to be aware of, but there's a different reason for their behavior. They promise assistance but then act like the demands are unfair when it comes to the point of managing. They tell you how happy they are for their help, and then act as if you're burdens. It's yet another attempt to sabotage your own values. According to you they cause you to doubt the truth and alter your beliefs about what they feel is right for them.

They're experts in Guilt-Dumping

They are masters at making use of shame to gain gains. If you bring issues that annoy you, they'll make you feel embarrassed for speaking about the subject. It will make you feel guilty if you aren't careful, or for keeping your own self-deprecation and carrying about it. When you're faced with manipulators of your emotions, everything you do is utterly wrong and is your own blame, regardless of what problems you and your partner face.

They state the victim's spot

There is no responsibility for them when it is left to manipulators of emotions. If they do it, or attempt to do, it's the obligation of another person. Someone else is responsible for this, and it's now your responsibility typically. If you are annoyed or angry it's your responsibility to not have unreasonable expectations. If you are angry and you do not understand why, it's your fault to cause disruption. People who manipulate emotions are not able to show for.

They're Over the Top and Too Early

If it's a relationship that is intimate or a corporate arrangement the chances are that manipulators of emotions have missed a few key moves. They are too eager to are able to share and insist on the exact same things from you. They display the impression of vulnerability and sensitivity, but they are merely putting you in a trap. The trick is designed create a feeling of special as a person to be accepted into their circle of friends however, it's also designed to make you feel not only bad for yourself but also ashamed of their actions.

They're an emotional black Hole

Mental manipulators think they're geniuses in drawing by a certain set of emotions all around them. Everyone around them knows they're feeling down.

But there's a more important part. They're skilled enough that they can feel it but not everybody is conscious of their state. This leads individuals to feel guilt and pressured to take action to correct their manipulators' moods.

They're likely to choose to assist Maybe even Volunteer and behave like an Hero

A desire to help transforms into sighs grunts, and the suggestion that whatever they choose to do is a huge burden. And if you're shining the spotlight on your fear and they'll make it clear that they're not interested in you. ensure they're willing to be supportive, naturally since you're suspect. Target? to make you feel embarrassed to make you feel ashamed, embarrassed, or even insane.

They're just one-ups to you

Whatever issues you face It's worse for those who manipulate emotions. In telling you that their problems are more pressing they undermine the importance of your complaints. What message do they convey? There's no reason to open up, just shut it down and leave.

They know and they don't hesitate to hit all the Buttons

The manipulators of emotions are aware of the most vulnerable areas and can turn the facts against you. If you're unsure about your weight and weight, they're focused on the things you're doing and the fit of your clothes; If you're worried about an event coming up you're noticing how obnoxious and rude people are. Their sense of sensitivity is out of the question, and they use it to snare you, not to make you feel comfortable.

What are the best options for you?

If you're thinking of collaborating with someone who employs these methods in a personal or business relationship, you need to wise up. Since if you're continuously exposed to it and you're going to be paying an immense psychological price. Here are some things to think about.

It's Nothing to do with You.

Gather evidence to prove the diagnosis and then get external confirmation that you are not able to trust or deny the diagnosis. You don't.

Do not seek an explanation or a change in behavior

It's a dream But you're not likely to be able to attain it. And, even if you do, it's not going to be the case. It's going be anything they do and they'll get what they want in the future.

Do not try to play your own game with them

They'll be victorious. They won that long time ago. Since the beginning, they may have been tweaking their techniques to suit their needs, and they're excellentactually, extremely excellent. However, do not give in to the urge to live the game.

Establish Restrictions for Health and Safety Restrictions

Clear boundaries and limits are essential, especially in the context of the family or other reasons you must maintain the bond. It is possible that you will require assistance from a trustworthy person beyond setting boundaries in order to stick to these boundaries.

Sometimes it is the Exit Door is the most effective strategy.

It is important to learn from your mistakes and receive expert help in making a decision and an agenda if you're not sure. Do not let things drag into the background for too long, as your personal life as well as your individuality and potential are at risk.

Believing that Things Will Change

You should remain focused as you work to improve your health. It's not a straightforward issue, but it's true. On the other hand the life can be good beautiful, lovely, and truly beautiful. Take advantage of it.

How to protect yourself from emotional Predators

While manipulation doesn't cause harm or put the subject in immediate risk, it is made to trick and alter the mindset, thinking and perception of the person who is intended to be affected by an issue or subject It is advisable to safeguard you and your loved ones against it.

Social influence, for instance, teens being incorporated into a particular culture or society that allows interaction with other people at the workplace or at home is admirable. Any influence in society that recognizes the right and privilege of individuals to choose, without being threatened, is typically viewed as beneficial.

Social influence is considered to be a sin when individuals manipulate others into bending against others' wishes. The effect can be extremely damaging and is generally looked as fragile in nature.

What is Gaslighting?

Gaslighting is one form of mental abuse and is frequently employed by people who are narcissists. The term itself was coined in 1938 due to an act. The play depicts an individual who tries to drive his wife crazy by playing with the lighting in their home. The wife in the play attempts to explain the situation to her husband. He refuses to believe that the lighting in the home is not changing in any way. She starts to think about her own and then he takes control. He's making her laugh and this is an excellent illustration.

There are many people who have to deal with narcissists every day basis. However, it's astonishing how few people understand what gaslighting actually is. Gaslighting is among the most used tactics of a narcissist to gain absolute control and control over their relationship. It slanders their partner and forces them to think about every thought or idea that enters their heads.

Narcissists have enormous egos and have the ability to be loved by themselves. They will go to extraordinary efforts to get people to see them in a certain manner. They frequently tell stories of greatness and believe that no one is more impressive than them. The majority of narcissists are charming and are able to draw the attention of an audience quickly. This makes it very easy to fall prey to them and to allow them to take control over your life. The ability to spot a narcissist in the beginning is the best way to stop them.

How to deal with the consequences of Gaslighting

If you realize that you're in a situation of gaslighting The first thing you must do is get rid of the situation. It is important to recognize that this is a damaging type of psychological and emotional abuse. If you want to live a life free of gaslighting, then you'll need to decide to get out. It's not easy to make this choice on your own, but do not be afraid to ask for assistance. Talking to your loved ones or someone who is nearby, describing the circumstances, and seeking a solution can be your only option to get started on the path to healing.

It takes determination and courage to make the decision to leave a abusive relationship. If you're not yet ready, there are hotlines for abuse to help ease any negative feelings you have been experiencing. They can connect you to a number of resources that will assist you in removing yourself from the negative life you're currently living. In addition, they will be available to listen and help you begin to recognize and face the reality that you're the victim of being gaslighted.

The process of healing from the consequences of gaslighting isn't going to be a simple task to complete. This is particularly the case if you've been involved in a gaslighting incident for a considerable amount of time. It's likely that the trust you had confidence in yourself has completely diminished. It is possible that you don't believe in your judgement or mental sanity. After you've cut ties with the narcissistic gaslighter who dominated your life, you'll likely begin to ask yourself questions such as, what could you have done to not observed what was going on? In addition, you might be afraid of repeating the same mistakes again in your the next relationships, which can make it extremely difficult to move on.

Another way to deal with the consequences of gaslighting is to recover your own. It is probable that you are going to question your entire self-worth following an incident of gaslighting. From your judgement to your view of reality it can appear quite complicated. Sometimes, the amount of the abuse isn't important in the same way as the emotions that are left behind after it's over. It's important to recognize that if you don't believe in yourself, you might consider relying on others, which is normal However, being a victim of a relationship that was toxic, you must build confidence and trust in yourself which , in turn, will allow you to make the necessary changes in your direction. This is a path which is yours to choose and not the decision of someone else.

Journaling can be very helpful in coping with the consequences of gaslighting. The person who is suffering will undergo a variety of contradicting thoughts, emotions and beliefs. Journals can help the person to think and reflect on the areas of conflict between their own thoughts and feelings. This could be a mapping of the way you are feeling about the seeds you were set by the self-centered abused person in your life.

Meditation can be very beneficial to those suffering from gaslighting. It can help us calm ourselves and identify the trouble areas without judgement. Meditation can also help us to tune into our own inner being and connect with the piece of ourselves. When you're suffering from gaslighting, connecting to yourself can be challenging, and meditation can aid in the process. In addition to helping you reconnect with yourself, it will also assist in lower depression, anxiety, and general feeling of chaos.

Another thing that will assist you in coping with the consequences of gaslighting is to know more about the subject. You have clearly taken an important step towards the right direction by buying this book since it offers an abundance of information about everything connected to gaslighting. A continual search can aid in developing a stronger sense of yourself and provide you with greater understanding of the trauma you've experienced.

While going through the process of recovery, keeping your stress to a minimum feasible can be beneficial. Gaslighting is in itself very stressful, and when you're on the other side and feel stressed you are likely bring back the emotions you had in the gaslighting scenario. If you can lessen the stress that you experience this will enable you to release the negative feelings which gaslighting has caused to feel every when you're stressed.

The process of dealing with this is difficult , and it's an excellent idea to create a plan to ensure your safety when you are out of the abuser. Things like changing your phone number or informing your work colleagues of what's happening could help protect your partner from you. If you are in a situation where you fear the abuser hurting you or your family, you may request a restraining orders. If you're the only person living in the home changing the passwords and locks around your home can be beneficial.

If you've been the victims of gaslighting it's likely that you'll think that you are able to be reliant on the opinions of the person who abused you. You'll be questioned about what others are saying and wondering if the information is accurate or not. Rebuilding your trust in others isn't easy, but also feasible.

Being positive can be a fantastic method to recover from the negative consequences of gaslighting. When you have just emerged from the relationship that was abusive you are likely to find that you lack confidence in yourself or feel self-worth. Positive self-talk can help to restore your normal level of self-esteem as well as self-esteem. Writing down the things you appreciate about yourself, or things you are good at can create a positive image of yourself. Be sure to stay clear of the words that make you feel degraded or words that your narcissistic abuser would make use of.

Connecting to these individuals by joining a support network is very helpful in dealing with the consequences from being involved in a relationship with a high-stakes personality that used gaslighting techniques. Members of these groups will be willing to share their experiences and be able to offer some suggestions on how they got back to normal that might be helpful to you.

One final idea to help you get over gaslighting's effects is to concentrate on how you feel physically. If you're psychologically or emotionally damaged, it's very common to ignore the physical condition of your body. If you decide to put your focus back towards a healthier lifestyle it will positively impact your overall wellbeing. You'll feel more relaxed and feel more energetic, which will let you concentrate on non-physical aspects more quickly. Making sure you get daily exercise, eating a healthy nutrition , and sleeping enough makes it easier to concentrate on healing from the other negative effects of gaslighting.

Chapter 9: The Art of Brainwashing, and Other Mind Control Strategies

The first recorded usage of the term "brainwashing" was around 1950 during the Korean War and was soon became popular because the ideology encouraged fear, anxiety and other negative emotions in people of every creed, culture, and religions across the globe. This was utilized to describe the methods of manipulation employed to manipulate Korean as well as Chinese soldiers to alter the psychological state that of American prisoner of war who were under their command. While in the foreign camps of concentration POWs were subjected to different methods of brainwashing (most of them new and never tested before) until they renounced their identities, changed their the nationality of their country which was their home country, and admitted to war crimes in which they played no part. Since its introduction and its widespread recognition as a form of psychological development the practice of brainwashing has become an important point of reference for many , from those who would like to employ it, to people who wish to take back the control of their lives and also those looking to avoid the need to ever have to confront any form of brainwashing or other methods or motives. Although the term and its research might be relatively new in the area of psychological research, fundamental techniques and mechanisms that are used to induce brainwashing have been used since the time humans have attempted to alter how others behave, think and react. This book we're going to examine the science behind brainwashing, the basics of brainwashing, as well as how to stop it from being used as a weapon against you, especially by those who seek to cause harm.

The process of removing abrain is different from OTHER methods of controlling the mind.

Brainwashing isn't a new phenomenon in psychology, or within the human past as you examine the elements of the technique and how they've developed. It is often referred to in the context of "thought restructuring" for those who study it in depth; the name of the technique was given by the description of the method of brainwashing. It is defined as the deliberate alteration of the thoughts or feelings of a person or group of people without their consent (and usually without their conscious awareness). Methods of brainwashing are employed wherever you go, but often not for malicious or deceitful purposes. Certain methods are employed regularly in the advertising industry or even for political campaigns. Similar to manipulation and persuasion, it's hard to spot until you're fully immersed in the.

But, unlike the two methods, which also have deep connections to psychological research and Dark Psychology, brainwashing is not as effective unless extended to large numbers of potential victims (like political and religious cults).

Here's a quick overview of methods to help people who aren't familiar with the area of Dark Psychology to discern the differences:

It is. The use of persuasion when employed can be used to convince the person to believe that they have changed their mind through deliberate thought and increased perception of the situation. The people who make use of this technique would like their targets to undergo a an altered perspective which makes them feel better about the decision they made to change their thinking or behavior. They are looking to influence their future , without changing their past.

II. Manipulation is the successful transformation of thoughts and feelings through coercion and force in order to gain control over actions of one's in order to gain a naive and often motive that is malicious. The manipulator is not concerned with the past or the long-term prospects of their target other than what they must know to be able to control their targets to benefit.

III. The techniques of brainwashing fall between the two. They aren't always employed to harm others, but the term has gained notoriety due to its popularity among those who seek to make use of it as a method to gain control over other people. The principal goal of brainwashing is to allow the person doing the brainwashing (sometimes called"the agent") to induce the subject to change their thoughts and behavior to be in line with their core values and prior experiences to gain control over their thinking and behave. If used for ill-intentional or untrue motives the primary goal of brainwashing is to target the person's fundamental (their beliefs about who they really are as well as their beliefs and moral beliefs) and make them think about their beliefs to make sure they accept these new "truths" they've been exposed to as truth providing them with confidence or confirmation when they want to stabilize their lives.

The more subtle types of brainwashing have been successfully employed to promote tobacco products through subliminal messages that are embedded in TV shows, videos magazines, radio, and other channels. They might not be advertising exclusively for the item, but simple images of people smoking cigarettes and smoking as they live their lives. The brainwashing techniques utilized in this type of advertising for marketing had subtle but powerful elements like making certain that the person smoking the smoking cigarette in the image or video is always laughing and happy or picking the right colours and images to draw people into the scene and convince them to rush to the store to buy cigarettes.

STEPS FOR SUCCESS BRAINWASHING

Individual strategies don't make a difference when trying to manipulate other people. The process of brainwashing requires a carefully chosen method that is developed based on the desired of the method, its purpose, and the amount of time the individual must accomplish the goal, or methods of brainwashing. No matter what the particulars are the basic methods of brainwashing will be the same for those who are learning, practicing and perfecting their strategies.

It is. Rewrite the Past: The very first step is crucial in terms of successful brainwashing. Rewriting the person's story begins by making them question their beliefs, their past and everything else they've had to endure and consider the value of. If the person who is brainwashing cannot influence their audience to think about their beliefs and believe, there is no way that they'll be capable (subconsciously or with force) to present new facts and beliefs. If someone begins to ask questions about their own beliefs and their beliefs, they're more likely to accept new ideas and begin to seek answers in their unfamiliar surroundings and form an unambiguous perception about the universe.

II. Inspire Guilt: Guilt can be an effective emotion that brainwashers employ to force the victims to alter their thoughts, feelings, and behavior patterns. At the end of the first stage the target is expected to ignore everything they've ever believed or learned (assuming the brainwashing process will follow be a plan) and start to speak new ideas and concepts that their agent would like them to accept. They might be reluctant to keep embracing new ideas or modify their behaviour in complete ways however, as soon as they do not just reject their old beliefs, but find themselves feeling bad about their previous beliefs, they become less hostile and more receptive to future thoughts and manipulation of perception.

III. III. All is Lost Moment: It is a frequent occurrence among authors and storytellers who wish to create an emotional moment that their characters must overcome. "All is Lost Moment" occurs when "All Is Lost" is when a person finds themselves in a state of despair about:

A) who they are as well as their personality and their view of the world.

B) What they've been through and what they did in order to become the person they are today (the person they doubt and have lost all confidence in).

C) What they would like to see in the future and how they plan to get there, if any.

One of the risks of brainwashing until despair is the possibility of suicide for the victim or the chance that they could cause harm to others after losing the interest in human beings.

IV. Reaching out and making an offer: Brainwashing can be very lonely for the victim even though they are part of the same group. After they've been psychologically ruined until they are in desperation (certainly at this point in any successful brainwashing program) this offers the agent to build an emotional bond, whether superficial or not, in order to build confidence in them and allow the final shift from their current state of mind to the way of thinking or behavior that the agent wants to. This first connection is achieved by anything as simple as giving them a refreshing drink of water, a second portion of food, or something that they enjoy. It is a way to show (however hidden) empathy to the victim, and can make them more willing to engage in dialogue or even engagement. An gesture of kindness or compassion moment can transform an individual from being a threat to potential all-weather ally.

The V. Confession and desire to be involved to figure to make a difference or change an issue, people think about anything that will make to feel better and reassure them that they're making the right choices. In this moment the victim is dependent on the agent , and has no chance of breaking free prior to the scheme coming to an end and the consequences that are triggered. They might still be suspicious that they're being controlled however, they are more susceptible to convincing and other techniques to influence their brains in the event that the mechanism is enhanced.

VI. Recognizing and Rebirth. In the final phase, the person completely accepts the process of brainwashing is able to accept the new reality they are presented with and transforms into the person they were programmed to become through a rigorous training manipulation, coaching, and even physically abused (not necessarily brainwashing techniques however, they are often employed in criminal, military, political and other shadier purposes).

When all of these methods are implemented to the fullest extent (or the most effective according to the situation) The brainwashing process may be considered successful and the agent could have an examination of the list of strategies which have been employed to determine how effective they've proved. Psychological research has revealed that brainwashing is among the least effective methods of control over emotions and mental state that people should put their time since it's complex, and the real effects of all of the techniques are not yet studied thoroughly. The primary issue which researchers are asking about brainwashing techniques from the beginning is whether it's as efficient as a manipulative tool as many people believe it to be (worry or think that it is) due to the mechanism of brainwashing itself or due to the vulnerability of individuals to psychological manipulation. Then, they pose questions like: what is it that makes some people more vulnerable to psychological manipulation than other people? Do existing strategies to brainwash people work? Can they be employed across different ethnicities, genders and social categories in the same way like other people, or will the same factors and methods be transposed?

PUBLIC BRAINWASHING Strategies used in GENERAL and DARK PSYCHOLOGY

A typical brainwashing technique in various contexts and industries is the constant reinforcement of the notion or belief they want the victim accept. This is accomplished through techniques that are auditory, like listening to a repetitious music track; or by using verbal methods that include requiring victims to repeat a phrase over and over until it is all they speak of; or by placing it into the form of a video that is then repeated repeatedly as the sole source of light or sound source in the victim's confinement zone. Another option is to have an individual surrender their logical thinking process and instead rely on their emotions to make their decisions about their thoughts and actions. The emotional reactions may be triggered by various factors like defense against fear of being excluded or violent outbursts triggered by the person being so angry or annoyed from the person they are dealing with that they strike out instead of taking the time to breathe and contemplating any request or action. One of the ways that agents can accomplish this is to take the time to constantly make their targets confused by offering their target information in snippets (which could or might not be the case) until they reach a level that they are intrigued. The withholding of information helps keep the audience coming back to them in order to learn more and believe that they're expanding their knowledge about the universe. They are more prone to manipulation once an agent has the ability to start the brainwashing cycle with full force.

Coercion and emotional control are the most common methods used to brainwash typically after the agent has gained confidence of their target and is now able to proceed with their plan. This method involves altering the psychological state of their targets either through creating anxiety or stimulating the recall of painful incidents until the target becomes so exhausted from emotional stress that they cannot acknowledge that they have been manipulated or even recognize that something is not right. Expertly trained brainwashing professionals can create a feeling of security for their client through their presence or their willingness to sit and examine their personal issues, especially in the case of someone who isn't able to openly divulge their thoughts and feelings to anyone else.

CONSEQUENCES of BRAINWASHING on individuals and groups

The results of brainwashing (and the power it has as a method of manipulating the mind) have been challenged by a variety of groups of scholars as well as analysts that have studied for years American troops who upon they returned to United States after being liberated from prisons during war were found to be the victims of brainwashing. They believed that the people who they spoke to were likely to be influenced by physical violence and neglect, not through the actual methods of brainwashing. One of the main reasons for believing this is that of the tens of thousands of prisoners who have gone through the brainwashing process, less than two dozen have made any improvement. But, this number only includes the soldiers who decided to go back home to United States and not those who were so infuriated by their homeland that they chose to remain in the country of their captors, even after the war was over and were released.

Cults from all over the world have played an important part in brainwashing and the consequences due to their ongoing involvement. From a distance it is easy to claim that cults are bizarre and difficult to understand why someone would ever want to be actively involved. But, coercion, brainwashing and other methods of psychological dominance are frequently employed by people who are members and recruiters in these organisations and are among of the most researched and tested agents and manipulators of society. The most effective method they use to achieve their goals is by exploitation those most susceptible to manipulation, by making them feel special and a part of a community and then influence them through deceitful sympathy or convincing them that the thing they advocate for is legitimate and morally acceptable.

Effective brainwashing may have a variety of long-term consequences for individuals and groups of individuals. The most well-known negative side effects that are alleviated or eliminated by the process of removing brainwashing (more generally referred to deprogramming) are:

I. A shaky sense of confidence: This is often a cause for an array of challenging and destructive behaviors like dependence to alcohol, or use of potent substances.

II. Inability to trust people Individuals who have managed to get out of the cycle of brainwashing (successful or not) seem to retreat into their own selves and cannot believe in anyone they meet following their experience, regardless of whether it was an acquaintance or someone they love with all their heart.

III. Every test is a test After a period of brainwashing the majority of our lives is prone to losing its excitement. The person who is affected no longer takes part in the activities were once their passions They lose all enthusiasm and optimism for the future. If they're given the chance to take part or be involved in an activity then they take a step back and scrutinize the entire details before deciding if it is something they would like to participate in.

Chapter 10: Utilizing NLP (Nlp) to influence people

Neuro Linguistic Programming, or NLP is the method that the human brain creates a reality based on sensory information, emotions and words that are put into tangible examples. The examples are then used by the intuitive mind to decide the best way to respond to situations physically and internally.

A thorough understanding of this process lets a person to construct their own reality. It may seem rather shocking to the non-resisting person, but its purpose is due to science as we become more acquainted with the way the human mind functions. If someone is in a situation that might not yield positive outcomes The ability to alter the outcome in a split second is an amazing asset.

Illustration frameworks are based on abilities of each individual and how they is able to adjust and process the new information. Some prefer to think about it, while others want to discuss it, and some may prefer for it to "feel" the experience. Based on the individual's way of life, directing them in a similar manner could affect them in your own mind. You're promoting a similar idea or concept, but you're doing it in a way it sounds appealing to them.

The results that are very well-framed are achieved by clearly defining the most desirable results and then communicating the results in an optimistic light. Instead of listing what you do not need be clear about what you actually require. If you can have your desired results clearly defined and defined, you'll need to present your thoughts a thought-setting process by picturing the outcome in relation to physical objects you might be able to comprehend. For instance, you'll have to visualize the sound of someone's voice, the general hum you'd like to hear, or any smells or other objects you could discover once the goal has been achieved.

Sharing the results with others in this manner allows them to benefit and keep them to the forefront of your mind. Making your best outcome persuasive enough to other people will make them want to achieve the same goal. A lot of publicists make use of this method to entice customers to buy their product by describing what their life will be like in the event of purchasing the product. The representation entices the customer to "see" the goal of a happy life.

The ability to show greatness is another technique employed within the NLP umbrella. When you show yourself as an individual who is successful or by examining someone else who has made it and success, you take on their belief system and world. Additionally, you gain insight of the reasons they make the decisions they make and how their beliefs impact the decisions they take. If you are addressing someone using their convictions, you are guaranteed to convince them about the truthfulness of your ideas and ideas.

These techniques can be applied to a variety of situations and are increasingly being utilized in the world of business. What is the most effective one could be in the event they are able to influence the actions of their coworkers? Being able to influence all around you isn't an issue of control but an energy of cooperation that allows people to work together for a common purpose. Being able to have everyone in agreement and without a single desire on the highest priority ensures that the final result will be acceptable to all.

NLP is utilized in a variety of ways in the business world and one of its primary uses is to create an advantage over others. What would you like to be able to convey information in a way that allows you to seamlessly communicate whenever the need be felt by people at different levels of an organisation? What would you like to be able to convince someone to achieve something through the use of language patterns that are explicit? How would you like to be able to assist people in overcoming their challenges to increase their effectiveness and profit-oriented. What would you like to be able to influence the decisions of your customers by talking to them on a non-deliberate level to ensure they only get an enthusiastic response to your product or service or accept your suggestions?

NLP Communication Model

What is the process? If you think about it, NLP instructs you that all of us have certain predispositions based on the manner in which we think, and the way we communicate with the world and to ourselves. When we are able to be aware of the ways we perceive then it is possible to change the way we think.

For example. As a group, we have a favorite method of interpreting what is going within our lives and our thoughts.

We can either rely on our sense of sight, sound or touch. If we experience a particular sensation of sight, we can translate what we see into pictures within our minds. If we experience the sensation of touching that we like and touch, we can effortlessly create an inference of the feeling into our inner feelings and so on.

Let's say that we have a inclination to visual images, or seeing. This will become clearer as well as other things in the words we say, "see you later," "I am able to see this incident," "Out of the image and therefore not relevant" and so on. Every expression that includes the feeling of seeing.

If we do have the desire to make contact, we could make statements such as "look at you a second moment," "you can clutch this idea in your hands," "I have an optimistic vibe whenever I think about it" any expression that evokes the physical sensation of touching or sensation.

In the event we do know this, we are able to listen to the words of people about themselves, and then we can figure out the preferred method of correspondence. It is possible to increase the oblivious effect on them using their preferred method of sending letters that they send back. We will therefore use phrases and words they utilize to achieve this.

Have you noticed that people have a tendency to like people who are similar to them? Have you noticed that you and your friends have common pursuits? This is the method by which it operates.

Try this the next time you talk with them. Check their shoulders around when they breathe in and out, and then duplicate the movements. This way you breathe in, you breathe in, and when they breathe out, you breathe out. Note how this gives you an unintentional connection to them. They will not realize the mistake you made, but they will feel more and more connected with them and be more enthused about you subconsciously.

One of the most significant commitments NLP has made to self-awareness as well as life enhancement is its use in communication both within and out. NLP has a wide range of functional strategies that allow us to be part in more important interactions with others around us by removing many of barriers to effective contact. This article will take a look at a few ways that NLP can enhance our communication capabilities with others and thus improve the quality of our lives.

Also known as Neuro Linguistic Programming to provide an clarification, NLP is centered around the language patterns that are that are associated with the way that we communicate with each other and others. Language patterns, specifically the words we use and the way they are used, profoundly impact our daily life experience. If we meet with some kind and we mark this understanding, that name or the words we choose to use CHANGE the experience. For example, you come home from a day at Disneyland and someone asks you about the experience. You could answer that it was fantastic, amazing, thrilling exhilarating, thrilling, exciting, heart-siphoning or crazy... Whatever word you choose to use to describe your experience is the experience. Let's suppose you choose "frightening". In reality, the word "frightening" is just an amalgamation of letters. Yet, it's an act of faith, full of mental imagery and contemplation connected to that mixture of letters. Consider this: Can you imagine that you had no idea about the word "startling"? Because of some reason, it may have been omitted from your vocabulary or perhaps you'd never ever heard of it when you were a child. Okay, how can you people generally feel 'terrified'? It's explained by the fact that some small island nations do not have a term for war. '... Imagine how this impacts their life!

Words trigger compound responses within our brains. Things we say or hear spoken to us, particularly the language they are spoken in, trigger us to think in certain ways about certain things and react in particular ways to specific situations.

What would you say to someone who asks "How do you feel?"? Do you simply respond "Fine" or "alright". How would you feel after you said this? What do you feel afterwards after having made that statement?

Imagine a scenario in which you were asked "Remarkable! ", "Extremely Superb" or "Awesome. Are you able to imagine how you'd experience a sensation that is unexpected? Two people may have similar experiences each day, however, they can both mark them "alright" while the other can refer to them as "Great" and the result is that one feels wonderful and one will physically feel good.

Do you feel the power of the words?

If not, think about the issue in a gradually outside conversational setting. Let's suppose that someone has expressed their opinion on something and you reply "I don't know if I agree with you." "... You think that this will make them feel distinctly off and then you respond with "You're incorrect". Both answers have shown the same significance... you may not necessarily agree with them, however, the words you use trigger different responses, which greatly impact the bond between the two people. You get the idea that words influence the way we feel.

As a Life Mentor as well as an NLP expert. NLP is a revolutionary method that will help in achieving the results you want in every aspect that you live. Utilizing the process you'll have the chance to alter your goals to discover what you actually want and then the best way to get it!

1. Positive

What do you require? This should be expressed in a positive way since your subconscious personality isn't aware about the difference between positive and negative

Did you know that living in a negative environment can cause harm to your health!

2. A tangible explicit

How will you know when you've had it?

What do you plan to do with it once you have it?

What will you experience what will you hear, feel and see the moment you experience it?

3. Contextualized

What time and place are you hoping to receive it?

What is the best time to not require it?

4. Self-achievable

It is vital that your goal must be within your personal zone of influence for instance. is something that you are in the power to influence.

What assets should you be able to use to achieve it?

What should you do to get it done?

Are you able to accomplish this could do yourself? But, does it require other people to continue to work with a particular objective with a specific goal in mind?

5. Natural

What are the advantages and weaknesses? There are always issues when the process of implementing an improvement. being aware of these makes you from being 'at-cause' when making a choice.

What are the benefits of introducing this enhancement?

What are the disadvantages of the introduction of this enhancement?

What are you doing to make this happen?

What do you? Become?

6. Beneficial

This is the motivation question. What qualities of yours will you achieve this goal?

What is the most important thing to you in receiving it?

What can this goal do to help you to abstain from feelings?

What's the benefit of this goal?

7. The first step

Do you have a starting step? To transform your dream into a concrete fact, you need to take the first step and without it, you'll be unable to get enough speed for you to reach the next step.

Make use of NLP to make changes and shifts for other people during ordinary conversations

Engaging in conversation with others is a crucial skill which very few people are prepared to master. Since people process and learn information in a way that is not expected the way you communicate may differ from the one whom you're speaking to. The difference in styles of correspondence often leads to misinterpretations and strong emotions.

Think about the possibility that you could quickly establish a connection with anyone. If you find yourself feeling awkward when meeting new people, you're not communicating effectively and may be losing connections you normally compensate for. The ability to form connections with someone lasts the majority of your day. Business, personal and casual connections are all affected by your ability to communicate in a manner that is easily understood and generally accepted.

NLP provides a variety of methods which allow you to share what you are thinking about in order to soothe your partner. If they are not in a relaxed viewpoint, they'll become more open to your thoughts and ideas.

Animals in the world have almost no communication with each other through the use of the spoken language. Only humans rely on spoken words to convey our thoughts feelings, emotions, and thoughts general perspectives. When watching other living creatures It can be clear that there's a debate taking place that we do not know about, yet they clearly comprehend the message. For those who aren't aware We also have an implicit conversation that can be used to communicate our views to others. What we call non-verbal communication is often ignored or ignored. NLP makes use of this language on a regular basis to build the feeling of affinity and recognition.

It is done by discretely monitoring the non-verbal communications of the other party. Once you have a feel of their manner of interacting, their personality and style of speech and conduct a process of coordinating and reflecting the manner of speaking they use. The question strongly suggests that we are drawn to people who have the most similarities to us. If you imitate the actions of someone else is a way of easing that person , and making the person you are talking to more open to relaxed conversation. In this way they'll be tuned into what you want to say with a positive view and may be positively changed.

Implanted directions are the questions which lead to a suggestion of an idea or thought which is then firmly rooted in the mind of the audience member. The question which begins with "What could it be?" ..." will make people imagine their response before they speak the answer. By presenting an idea in a setting, you can make it real and by asking these kinds of questions you're providing your audience with a new perspective and altering their belief frame.

Despite the fact that NLP can be seen as a method of training used to control and manage It should be utilized to make an effective tool for improving your life and the people around you. When used in a positive manner, NLP can decidedly change your life and the lives of the people you interact with frequently. The positive impact of NLP reduces tension and strengthens relationships.

Chapter 11: What is Brainwashing Works

In during the Korean War, Korean and Chinese captors were said to have trained American POWs within prison camp. A few detainees later admitted to having engaged in germ warfarebut they didn'tand pledged to communism at the conclusion of their detention. There were at least 21 soldiers who were unable to return into America. United States when they were released. This may sound amazing, but critics argue that it was only 21 from more than 20,000 people held within communist nations. Is brainwashing really effective in any reliable manner?

In the field of psychology the research of brainwashing, commonly called idea reform, is a part of the realm of "social influence." Social influence occurs all the time. It's the array of methods to influence their beliefs, attitudes and behaviors. For example, the "compliance" technique seeks to create a tangible shift in someone's behavior and does not focus on the person's beliefs or attitude. It's an approach that is known as the "Just Do it" method. Persuasion, on the contrary side, is designed to bring about an actual change in your attitude and/or "Do it in the way that makes you feel healthy/happy/well/effective." The method of education (which is known as"propaganda method" when it's not the only option) "propaganda method" in cases where you don't believe what you're being taught) uses the social-influence gold, attempting to bring about a shift in the individual's thinking that go beyond "Do it because you believe it's the right best thing to do." The practice of brainwashing is one of the most serious forms of social influence that utilizes all these methods to influence the mind of a person without the consent of the person and generally against his will.

Because brainwashing is an insidious form of influence and impact, it demands total isolation and trust of the person being targeted which is the main reason you learn about brainwashing in prisons as well as totalist cults. The person who represents (the brainwasher) must exercise total control over the person (the person being brainwashed) to ensure that the patterns of sleep eating, the use of the bathroom , and the fulfillment of the other human necessities are dependent on the decision-making and will of their representative. The process of brainwashing is where the representative takes away the person's identity until it is no longer effective. The representative is then able to replace it with a new set of attitudes, habits and beliefs that function in the present environment of the target.

Although most psychologists believe that brainwashing is feasible in the right conditions However, there are those who believe it is unproven or at best as a less severe type of influence than what that which the press portrays it as. Certain definitions of brainwashing demand the possibility of physical injury, and according to these definitions, most extreme cults are not practicing genuine brainwashing as they usually don't physically assault their recruits. Others rely in "nonphysical pressure and control" as an equally effective method of claiming influence. Whatever meaning you're employing, a lot of experts are of the opinion that, even in optimal conditions for brainwashing the results of the process tend to be temporary. The victim's previous identity isn't actually removed by the process instead, it's hidden until it is over, the "new identity" is no longer being cultivated, the old mental and values will come back.

There are psychologists who believe that the apparent transformation of American POWs during the Korean War was the outcome of abuse that was commonplace rather than "brainwashing." In reality, the majority of POWs during those days of

Korean War were not converted to communism in any way which is why there is the question of trustworthiness is brainwashing a method that has comparable outcomes across different cultures and personalities or does it depend heavily on the vulnerability of the target to being influenced? In the next part we will examine an expert's explanation of the process of brainwashing and determine the characteristics that make a target easy to identify.

In the 1950s In the latter half of the 1950s, the psychologist Robert Jay Lifton studied former prisoners from Korean War and Chinese war camps. He concluded that they had experienced a complex process which began with assaults on prisoners' sense of self-worth and concluded with what was believed to be a transformation in the way they thought. Lifton finally outlined a sequence of procedures that were involved in the cases of brainwashing which he studied

Attack on identity

Guilt

Self-betrayal

Breaking point

Leniency

Obligation to acknowledge

The burden of regret

The release of guilt

Harmony and growth

Final confession and renewal

Every one of them happens in a secluded environment which means that the fact that all "typical" social references are absent, as well as ways to reduce the impact of mind-clouding such as inadequate nutrition and sleep deprivation are usually an element of the process. It is common to find the presence or the constant risk of physical injury that can contribute to the victim's difficulties in thinking critically and independently.

It is possible to roughly break down the process Lifton has identified into three stages that include breaking through the self opening possibilities of redemption and then rebuilding the self.

The self is being broken down.

Identity Assault Identity: You're not the person you think you are. This is a deliberate attack on a person's sense of self (also known as his identity or self-image or) and the core beliefs. The person who represents the target negates all that defines the person they are: "You are not a soldier." "You don't belong to a person." "You aren't protecting flexibility." The person who is being targeted is constantly under attack for weeks, days, or even months to the point where he's exhausted, confused and lost. When this happens, the target's convictions are less convincing.

It's a shame that you are guilty. As an identity crisis has begun being ingrained into the target, the representative simultaneously creates an overwhelming feeling of guilt within the target. He constantly and relentlessly criticizes the subject for every "sin" the person has committed, no matter how tiny. The target may be criticized for any and every thing, including his "evilness" in his opinions to eating in a way that is too slow. The person being targeted is beginning to feel a anxiety, feeling embarrassed, that whatever the person does is wrong.

Self-betrayal: I agree with you that you're a bad person. After the person becomes confused and sunk in guilt, the person in charge asks him (either in the event of physical harm or continuing mental assault) to attack off his family, friends and colleagues who have the identical "really wrong" conviction system that he believes in. This denial of his personal convictions and the those he feels a strong sense of loyalty will increase the guilt and loss of identity that the person who is being targeted is already feeling.

The breaking point Where do I belong? Where am I? And what do I need to do? In the midst of a dilemma about his identity with deep shame, having renounced what he been a firm believer in for so long, the person may experience what is referred to as"nervous breakdown. "nervous disorder." In the field of psychology "anxious break down" is actually an assortment of signs that may indicate any of a number of mental disorders. It could be accompanied by uncontrollable crying or depression, as well as general confusion. The person in question may be losing touch with reality and feel of being completely lost and lonely. Once the person reaches the threshold of snapping the sense of his identity is in danger of being taken awayas he lacks a any idea of who he is or what's taking place to him. The agent creates the opportunity to change to a new belief system that can help the victim escape his suffering.

The possibility of salvation

Leniency: I can help you. When the target is in a state of confusion The agent might offer small gesture of kindness or a reprieve from the violence. The agent could offer the person an ice-cold drink or perhaps ask the victim what he really feels he is missing from returning home. In a state of devastation that is the result of a continuous mental assault, the tiny kindness seems significant and the person receiving it could feel a sense happiness and satisfaction that are completely beyond the offer, just as if the person has given him a life.

The need to confess The answer is that you can take care of yourself. For the first time during the process of brainwashing the person being targeted is confronted by the contrast of anxiety and guilt of the identity attacks and the sudden relaxation of acceptance. The victim may have an urge to show appreciation for the kindness extended to him. At this moment, the agent might suggest confession as a way to alleviate regret and intense hurt.

The directing of guilt is why you're hurting. After months or weeks of confusion, assault or breakdown, and then a moment in a state of relaxation, victim's regret is meaninglessand he is unsure of the error he committed He feels that in his bones that he's doing something wrong. It's like an empty slate, which lets the agent fill the gaps by affixing the guilt, that feeling or "wrongness," to whatever they want. The agent ties the victim's sorrow to the beliefs system that the agent is making an effort to change. The person being targeted begins to believe that it's his beliefs that are the source of his shame. The difference between old and new is established: The previous belief system is linked to psychological (and usually physical) discomfort; while the new system of belief is linked to the possibility of getting rid of the pain.

Conclusion

Psychology-based warfare is in use for many thousands of years. It's been used to create fear in the adversaries as well as to boost or decrease morale, or to intimidate or even to inspire entire nations and to mobilize soldiers. The most effective type of psychological warfare occurs that the target doesn't know it's happening. From Ancient civilizations through the Cold War, to the War on Terror. Psychological warfare has utilized tools and strategies built on the study of human behavior and thought. The brain is an effective weapon as well as a vulnerability if it is controlled in a defensive and offensive manner.

You might also have seen the techniques or methods you know someone has employed on you or on others.

If you read about the experiences of archetypical characters who utilize specific techniques or methods, do you relate to them because you've utilized the same strategies? Maybeyou've realized that you might be a victim by someone who has employed these methods on you. If you're feeling shocked or even guilty You're not alone. The book is not intended to "call out" errors or advise you how to recognize people who could profit from you, or even to simply guide users on how to employ these methods to gain selfish benefits. The goal was to provide an overall overview of the world of research of dark psychology, the techniques employed to study dark psychology. It also explains ways to employ these methods and also ways to protect yourself from those who practice. It was just a small taste of the dark side. can be.

Certain aspects of these abilities or methods that are ingrained into our lives. they have influenced our thinking or actions, and we've frequently used these techniques occasionally. We didn't know or even notice these methods or tools in use until we were aware of these methods, similar to how this book might have given you the information. Many of us did not realize that we're an "triangulator", "blaster" or "projector" and maybe an "flirt". We were using certain methods. In the moment, they was natural, like it was automatic. For certain people the skills seem similar to breathing. Certain strategies could have become routine due to interactions with our surroundings for instance, watching people close to us, such as relatives, friends or even a significant person. Perhaps , we observed someone whom we consider to be to be a role model or famous person we admire employ exactly the same approach.

www.ingramcontent.com/pod-product-compliance
Lightning Source LLC
Chambersburg PA
CBHW071836080526
44589CB00012B/1017